THE EDGE OF A BUSINESS

THE EDGE OF A BUSINESS

BUSINESS

Battles, Lessons and Mind Games

ABDULRHMAN ALHAZMI

Book Design: Opeyemi Ikuborije

ISBN: 9798848809879

CONTENTS

FORWARD

I write this book in honor of my parents and family, who have encouraged me to be the best version of myself. I was raised in a well-educated family, allowing me to live through experiences that any kid wish for. My parents accepted me for who I am, supported me through my business journey, and were there when I needed them.

To my sisters, who listened to me when I rumbled about business and life, believed in my capabilities, and brainstormed ideas with me. Thank you for being the sisters a brother could dream of.

I also wrote this book to the coach, who encouraged me to start writing this book five years ago. I still remember him questioning my perception of who should write books. Thank you for instilling confidence in me and pushing me toward achieving my goals.

To my Family: I love you and hope I can repay you with a fraction of what you have given me.

INTRODUCTION

When I was ten years old, I saw cars piling up at the gas stations waiting for their turn to fill up their car tanks. So I dreamt I would own a gas station one day, and I noted that in my diary to remind myself of that dream. I dreamt of the cars and stores that would open their shops and collect rent. In reality, I had a passion for business.

My first business venture was in elementary school when the school decided to do an open day. Students who participated in the open day had to sell a product, which could be food, service, or any product. So my cousins and I decided to sell Macdonald's burgers. We bought a bunch of big macs and sold them with a margin of profit. Kids our age loved big macs and we were sold out in a couple of hours, but as natural entrepreneurs we were not satisfied and so we went to Macdonald's and bought more burgers with the profits we made and sold them all. That experience was so enriching as a young kid who knew nothing about business except buying and selling what people would be willing to pay extra for. We were not geniuses to know that.

Fast forward to high school, my parents wanted a better education for me, and I was sent to study at a boarding school in Lebanon. I went to Lebanon and did not know anyone there, nor had relatives to lean on if I needed to. I was a teenager still trying to cultivate myself and build my character. I have many stories and memories in Lebanon that I won't go through in this book. But, if there is a place that I wish to visit again in the nearest future, it would be the abandoned Lebanon (Covid-19, corruption and economic policy have somewhat destroyed Lebanon).

After graduating from high school, I went to the states to attain my bachelor's degree in Mechanical Engineering from Pennsylvania State University. I was so mature by then, and the experience of living in a new place with few people to know was not new to me since I went through the same experience in high school. In college, I was very focused on my studies and cautious about making any decisions that would jeopardize my graduation. I knew that life is all about decisions we may create or are destined to live.

After graduating, I was proud to have overcome the challenges of living abroad since I was 14 years in high school till attaining my college degree. I can still picture that young teenager living all alone and making so many mistakes that could have halted his development to be the man he aspired to be. Life's many distractions could take you away from your values. But, we must stick to what we believe is right. Life is short, and we will have so many regrets if we do not live it in the best means.

When I started writing this book, I wanted to share my humble learning experience with aspiring entreprenewurs. I aimed to let readers know how I felt when I was lost and how I overcame my struggles. I wanted readers to reflect on the ups and downs of a young entrepreneur. I thought that people would associate more when they hear the story of a business in the form of a journal because I wanted the same when I started my entrepreneurship journey. The book is written in the form of a journal where I document my journey in business, learning experience, and aspirations.

12/07/2016 is the day I started blogging my thoughts. Five months ago, when I joined the biggest company in the world. Deep down, the job did not fulfil my ambition. I knew that there was a much better place waiting for me. I felt trapped in a hole, waiting for the payday to be deposited at the end of the month. From the first day at work, I started looking for a business idea of my own. I looked for products, and products brought ideas. Ideas generated dream work environment. I dreamt of having happy and ambitious employees supporting me to build a successful business. But dreaming without really achieving my goals was not an option. I started reading books about giant entrepreneurs like Phillip Knight (founder of NIKE), Ray Kroc (founder of Macdonald's), and Isadore Sharp (founder of Four Seasons). Great books written by very intriguing characters. I am sure that many might have heard the names behind these worldwide brands for the first time.

I started blogging today because it was the time to share my aspiration to join the world of entrepreneurship. My mind is continuously thinking, creating, and developing. I had to pursue an idea that would generate cash and then start to follow my dreams. I did not dare to quit. I was afraid of what the world was hiding from me. I was scared to reach a wall that would make me regret taking the risk. I needed someone to push me hard.

My work environment is toxic. When I first reported to work, I was enthusiastic and ready to disrupt and generate value. However, giant corporations' bureaucracy and standards were not aligned with my energy. I remember having a fantastic supervisor who has seen a lot in me. I decided that my time should be spent where I want to be for the next 20 years, which fuels my interest to work harder. I will establish a business if I like reading business news more than politics and sports. If there is a product that I like, I will start selling it.

One thing that surprises me is when people say they want to work in a company that offers the highest salary. Because the reality is salaries will not matter if you do not like the work you do for the next 25 years. You do not want to work in a place where you will wait for 25 years to retire. Take action and create your own business. Be the first person to attend work because you love what you do, and you will stop at nothing but to accomplish the startup's goals because it is your startup.

CHAPTER 1

WORK OR BUSINESS?

12/27/2016

My courage hasn't yet exploded my ambitions. I am still waiting for that drive to achieve financial freedom and travel to the world of entrepreneurship, where everyone is ambitious to pursue whatever they seek.

Today, I was reading a book on Elon Musk, one of the leading entrepreneurs of our time. And, I found that after Paypal was sold to eBay for more than $300 million, Musk invested all his money in three other startups – Tesla, SpaceX, and SolarCity, which was worth an investment close to $200 million. That is a lot of money to risk on a startup. The companies are worth trillions nowadays.

The economy in Saudi is crashing, and everyone is pessimistic about what the future holds for us. Economists are also projecting a very steep suffering economy. But, I would say these times should be encouraging, and every time, there are opportunities. Follow your guts.

12/29/2016

The last week of 2016 was the most depressing. 2016 is folding up, and I am still struggling with whether I should continue working or quit and focus on my Goals. You must overcome three habits to achieve your goals – determination, patience, and change.

While traveling from Dammam to Riyadh (approximately a 4-hour drive), I listened to motivational speeches for almost three hours. I was trying to figure out the setbacks preventing me from accomplishing my dreams. Why do I feel like living in the land of slavery where people did not believe they had choices. And I came up with two reasons I would call excuses. The first excuse is money. I have a comfortable salary and save almost 70% of my total income. The second obstacle is the pressure from people around me. I am sure whoever will read this will struggle with the same problem. I decided that money won't be a problem if I could work as a part-time driver seeing I would have flexible working hours. This way, I could spare more time to work on my goals in the mornings and complete any commitments requiring morning hours when I am the most productive.

I have broken people into categories; opinions I care about and opinions that don't matter. My parents and sisters are the opinions I need to support my decision. I still think they will be shocked and disapprove of my intentions to quit. They will be mad and stubborn to comprehend my path forward. They will classify depression as being lazy and the drive toward failure. They will tell me that my job is many people's dream. They will tell me that I am making the mistake of my life and that I will regret it every day, and the list goes with discouraging thoughts.

Today, I was given a significant evaluation by my supervisor at work. I should feel enthusiastic to accomplish such an evaluation, but my emotions weren't near excitement. I felt like I was cheating myself, believing I could work hard at my job and achieve my goals. The supervisor tried to inspire me to work harder, as the subsequent evaluation would be more challenging, and told me, "I believe in your potential." I knew without a doubt that I would reach further than expected if I had the motive to continue working in the company. My supervisor liked me a lot, and I always enjoyed listening to his work experience and life pearls of wisdom. I resembled him like an older brother.

I had the wheels to rise high on the employment ladder, but the wheels did not have a driver.

After long consuming thoughts, I concluded. If you don't have the motive to put in more hours into what you do, then find something else and don't let that misery eat you up. We either choose to live our dream today and tomorrow or wait until the time has passed and no slice of the market cake is left for us to eat. Don't watch people achieve your dreams, be the one to achieve them. If you spend hours of your working hours thinking of opportunities that will satisfy your ambition, then don't complain and start working on fulfilling them.

"The struggle to achieve ambition is far more satisfying than the misery of job security at an organization where employees are unaware of the company's vision."

Tomorrow will be tough. But, my mind is determined to use that pressure hanging on my back to accomplish my ambition.

1/3/2017

Anyone who thought of resigning during an economic depression and lack of job opportunities would be considered "insane." I had a hard time figuring out the definition of insane. Is pursuing self-confidence and self-satisfaction insane? Is chasing your dreams insane?

After deep and long thoughts, reading many books, and listening to motivational and self-improvement speeches. I decided to quit my job and RUN for my dreams. At approximately 5:30 am, I walked up, took a shower, and this fear came pounding on my heart as if I was standing from the start line of a failed race. I started asking myself, "When will you have that courage to step up and follow your dreams? When?!" I felt that inspiration and courage as I went to my supervisor's office, a great person to learn from and work with. I came in, forgetting most of what I had planned to say. I started conveying my plans to quit. Although I expected an "insane" reaction from my supervisor, his surprise was very well put in encouraging words. He tried to talk me out of it, but as he said, "I know whatever I just said is going out of the second ear."

I will lay down the reasons behind my resolution. When I joined Aramco, I had dreams and goals. I had plans to achieve them, but throughout my daily job, I became a procrastinator. And, every day I wake up to go to work, I feel like I am going to the dentist. I needed my mind to be driven, no matter how small my goals or business ideas were. I needed to stop that self-talk. Am I doing the right thing working on a full-time job, or should I quit? Another reason is to have the working environment I desire and strive for. I will not submit to working in an environment because of security. I want to give 100% of my time to my dreams and goals.

To the reader: What I have written is my experience and evaluation of the situation. I will not tell you when to quit, and no one should. It should come from you. It took almost four months to listen to and analyze my inner self. A study once reported that many youngsters in Saudi Arabia are happy with their current positions. And so, you might be on the other part of the pie and wondering what to do. I encourage you to bring a piece of blank paper. Write down your goals on one side of the paper and how you would embed them in your daily routine to achieve your goals. As Warren Buffet says, "you have got the minds; just develop the habits."

"Just start and develop the habits."

1/8/2017

I came once again to my supervisor to inform him of my final decision to quit and move on. And he vigorously suggested taking a vacation for a month and keeping the job. I hesitated with my decision and agreed to take the vacation. At that moment, I feared failure, as if my knees were crippled. I walked to the bookkeeper and asked him to sign me for one month of vacation. My caring supervisor sought an explanation and pushed me to know why I wanted to leave. I couldn't explain the discomfort and depression I am having because of the work environment. I couldn't elaborate on my displeasure with the work itself. I could not justify my drive to work on what I like and for as long as the job takes. I felt like I couldn't breathe because I lacked the courage to support my decision. I wanted to leave the Company's premises as soon as possible. I started thinking again, why quit when I can still have my job and work part-time on my business. I was so depressed that I had to watch some motivational videos to revive my beliefs. I started blaming people around me for my weakness. I felt that everything would fail, and I would not feel the security I have today without that job. Instead of telling myself, "I am successful," "I will be a millionaire," I was doing that negative self-talk. While writing this journal, my mind exploded because I wanted to be successful, and I was jumping around decisions. I wanted to feel free, hop on a ship not knowing where the ship would sail, and enjoy the sound of the ocean. I doubted the Intentions of my decision. I asked myself if the reason for quitting was the desire for relaxation. I started criticizing my personality.

I am writing this on paper, and I don't know if people will read it in the future. I started picturing motivational speeches as a misleading future. I needed someone to call to get some wisdom. I wanted to call my father, but I knew he would even push harder to convince me to stay and keep the job. They say you need to be determined to succeed, and I say determination with minimal experience is somewhat oolishh.

**"To survive, you have to be like a wildebeest.
Once it is born, it takes less than an hour
to learn to run from the lion."**

1/23/17

It has been a while.

A week ago, I got weak. I feared the consequences of quitting. Thinking in the way of security and my position as an employed young engineer with a house hasn't left my mind. The devastation and ambition killer would be if I were to leave for Riyadh because I would be in a toxic environment that doesn't thrive for success. The country is also going through a high unemployment rate and deep economic reform, which strongly contributed to my fear of failure. When working back where I left, I also decided to focus on the gains, not the drains.

Jumping around decisions is not healthy; the focus is on success. And, I can see that my quick decisions to accomplish my goals started for the sake of reaching the top of the mountain as fast as I could. When in reality, life is a bicycle. You will get to your destination if you ride fast and rest; otherwise, you will run out of water.

**"Business is risky, but taking it at the
right time is smart."**

CHAPTER 2

BEGININGS

2/10/17

I am working on a project that will be huge when executed the right way. The project is building a food truck that strives for customer experience, quality, and mobility. Yes, winter 2016-2017 is when food trucks became a trend. It was booming, and people liked the idea. I was intrigued by the idea because of two reasons. The first one was when my colleagues at work and I were complaining about the food provided in the cafeteria; we had no choice but to eat from the cafeteria, as we only had a half an hour break. And so, I thought to myself, what if food trucks were here at lunchtime only! New York then came to my mind. Trucks are everywhere, and they include serving people's desires.

The second reason was that I liked taking people's orders when working with one of the existing food trucks for free. People were happy to be served by a Saudi. I was inspired to serve people and spread the smile. I believe the food truck owner lost me as a great asset to transform his business into the best nationwide. I had so many ideas that customers would have loved. I had so many business strategies that would have revolutionized the food industry in Saudi Arabia. Almost all the Saudi restaurants focus on the normal customer who has a variety of food when he is out of work. But, when he is at work, he has no options. Many employees struggle to find something to eat because they don't have a restaurant that offers quality and tasty food.

I wanted to partner with someone in the industry to cut through all the initial challenges. I will grant this to the owner of the food truck that I temporarily worked with when he said, "try to build your brand with your product." I had no experience in cooking. My cooking was moderate to not tasty. But, I treated it as a lab experiment. I looked online for burger recipes and had my family try the experiment. They liked it all. And moved on to find a food truck manufacturer and designer.

I then found a young businesswoman looking for an investor who had a food cart that sold burgers inside her university. I will be honest; I wasn't impressed with her product. But, I was admired by the owner's young age, who struggled between studying and serving people. I asked her to improve her product as it is not what I am looking for. But, I thought having an ambitious young partner who established a business at a young age would be successful. So, we partnered and immediatedly started working hard to build a strong, well-established company.

2/24/2017

Time is running, and operating the business is coming to flourish. The truck will be done in less than two weeks. I am feeling this fear of failure. The feel of wrong calculations and unpredicted consequences. Many scenarios are floating in my mind. Marketing, presentation, design, employees, transportation… you name it. However, I am proud of myself for having reached this point, and instead of just bouncing ideas, I am executing and executing well. I learned that you could never be perfect. For instance, I stretched the budget to almost 25% of the initial capital invested in my project studies, just in case. Well, I am using it all, and shortage of a small amount for the operational cost. I have also given up on some design accessories to add an aesthetic look to the truck. I am also a little paranoid about the municipal registrations, as they have not exhibited any cooperation.

I am also working in Aramco. I am trying to learn as much as I can. Getting to work on time and doing my daily work without using the company's time for my business. However, some days, I had to leave to finish some governmental requirements. It is hard to play the engineering role in the morning and business man in the evening jumping around from one real estate office to another, searching for a restaurant for sale, negotiating prices, and making deals with suppliers. It was not easy, but it was fun. I now know real estate prices, great designers, and quality suppliers. I was always expecting hurdles, but today I fear what will happen tomorrow. And, I say to myself, "We will crush tomorrow, and whatever is hidden by tomorrow, inshallah."

"You are what you are because of gets into your mind"

Zig Zigglar

3/31/17

We started selling!!

In the past month, I was so busy that I did not have time to write my weekly progress. I have been going back and forth from Ras Tanura to Riyadh (4hours drive) every weekend to check the status of the truck manufacturing. I arrive in Riyadh on Thursday and will ride back on Friday because I have other commitments that need to be done and cannot be delayed. So, yeah, it was hectic. A week ago, the truck finished after constant follow-up and repairing. Ultimately, I wasn't satisfied 100% as it didn't meet my expectations. Working hard is what will fulfill your disappointments.

Battling with the municipality to get the registration was a headache for no reason to comprehend. The municipality required food trucks to have their business stores for food preparation. In reality, they added the requirements to minimize the number of trucks in the city. In other words, the more complicated it is for people to start a food truck business, the fewer people will be interested in the matter.

3/29 was the opening day. And, yes, for two days, we sold only 20 burgers. Why? For many reasons I will explain later. If I would express my feelings, I feel like I failed. I started to think about all the people I did not listen to. I began to think of all the books I have read and the lessons I have learned through the experience of successful entrepreneurs. Although it is too early to judge the success of a business, the feeling is devastating because I will be spending more money to see if the business will pick up its pace. However, I have spent enough money to build the business, and I don't want to spend more. It is like having a car that leaks, and you keep fueling the car. Blames for the failure of any business must be owned; otherwise, you will be running an investigation of who committed the problem and not what the problem is.

The room must be filled with inspiration and hope for a team to keep working. I can see the frustration in the employees' eyes, and I can't do anything about it because I, myself as a leader, am playing a role in the matter. Things will get better, but does the story include the food truck business, or does it end somewhere in the future. To Be determined...

The fear of failing is not just from the money aspect. It is also the fear of time wasted, being pictured by society as a failure because I entered the burger market that is known to be very competitive, and even people are complaining about it. Although I kept the whole business a secret from my relatives to reduce the pressure on my back.

I feel like I once again made the worst decision with no honest evaluation of the product itself. I decided quickly because I wanted to reach the top as fast as possible. However, I have no regrets because the experience was something that I needed to understand and learn about the business.

"Life is not easy, but setting goals will make it easy," "business is not easy, but having hands-on experience will make it a whole lot easier."

"Success depends on psychology"

Tony Robbins

1. Worst location
2. More than ten burger competitors in the event
3. People's reaction to the design; thinking it is an ice cream

4/2/2017

We have participated in a well-marketed event that we registered and paid for one month ago. The event is expected to be big and is attracting thousands of people. The event was the first of its kind in the region in terms of magnitude. It included many activities and brands of all kinds of retailers and F&B. The first day of the event was bad for us; we had the worst location, did not have a strategy to attract customers, and relied on the truck's aesthetics.

All I can say is we killed it in the next two days. The things we did to attract more customers:

1. We changed our location to a more live and compelling location
2. We created a better marketing strategy by distributing free samples, touring people through the truck's design, and explaining its idea.
3. Diversifying the workforce with a more friendly touch.

On our first day at the event, we desperately sold 2 to 4 burgers. For the next two days, we sold an average of 85 burgers a day. That is remarkable! I remember trying to understand if I had made a mistake in getting into a business with no piece of the pie left for us to eat. Thankfully, We stood up, pivoted our strategy a little, and successfully executed our plans. People's reaction to the design, food, service, interaction, and marketing strategy, was amazing. Yes, I felt like I screwed myself the first day. But after seeing the success of our improvements over the next two days and listening to customers' feedback, I can see that it is not the business itself that screwed us; it is the location that made it difficult for us to survive.

"Always pivot, do not give up easily."

**"Do not judge your decisions,
but look for ways to improve your gaps."**

4/14/17

Thursday, 4/13, we were invited to serve food inside STC Camp, the leading company in the Telecom industry. When we were invited, I was excited but also worried because the company asked me to bring less than 100 burgers when they have more than 400 employees in their office site. I was hesitant that it would be a successful visit because the company told us that many food trucks came and failed to continue for reasons such as customer dissatisfaction and low purchasing power. However, for the first day, we sold almost 89 burgers with revenue of 2000 Riyals in 4hrs work. Not only that, but STC employees' reaction was amazing and supportive of the quality of our product and requested us to be permanently located inside their campus. For your information, many trucks have tried to sell inside STC but did not survive from the first day. A coffee shop considered one of the dominating coffee stores in Saudi Arabia has also tried to survive but closed its' shop. The facts are scary. We succeeded on our first day. We will have to wait for our next visit to assess the market reaction.

**"Do not listen to the failures of others.
Listen to the market. It is usually more accurate."**

4/23/2017 9:00 AM

I am at work, and I cannot stop thinking of what we will face tomorrow to prevent failure. Two days ago, I went to a consulting session with a businessman from Kuwait who reached success with multiple businesses. The session was a marketing strategy he used to "help" young entrepreneurs build and improve their businesses. I paid more than $150 for the session, thinking I would have answers to all my questions. It turned out that the guy was trying convince young entrepreneurs to buy his company's services which had different bundles for aspiring businesses. It was an indirect scam. With all due respect to the person, one hour of my time plus money was wasted.

I raised many questions to clear my goals and reach my vision. Currently, the business is doing great. Is it going to continue? This is a question I don't have an answer to. I am afraid it will be temporary for two reasons. First, if we were asked to relocate, we would lose our customers, and we would be stuck, which is a high probability since the food truck industry is fairly new in the region and regulations are changing quickly. The second reason is the weather aspect. It is getting warmer, and as the summer gets on the way, I am not sure if customers will still come.

**"Consultations need to be carefully picked.
Not everyone has the intention of helping"**

5/1/2017

One month past our inauguration, and business is picking up. Our customer base is getting bigger and bigger. We are still struggling with the municipality to issue a permit for the truck. I have been going back and forth with their representatives to complete the procedures and fulfil the requirements. And, yes, technically, we are currently working illegally.

Our employees are also working illegally for us. We are doing well in terms of revenue. However, many obstacles could turn our revenue to zero.

1. Illegal location
2. Illegal employees
3. No Work Permit
4. When the truck generator (electricity producer) heats up, it shuts down.

Our plan to reach our goal cannot be accomplished with all these problems. Our business today is very fragile. If we face any of these problems, it could shut us down or drain our profit.

My days: I am grounding the ground up. Working almost 18 hours with 4 hours of sleep and 2 hours commuting. I have thoughts of quitting. Thoughts of picking the wrong business are pounding in my mind. Thoughts of wasting my energy on something that won't have a huge return in the future. On average, I eat one and a half meals a day. I am losing weight. Many of my habits to success are compromised due to lack of time (working for 18 hours). I hope that my drive to make the business successful by hustling and grinding. What is the destination of my hope?

**"Lack of time. Lack of sleep.
Lack of social life. Hope is your drive."**

CHAPTER 3

CHALLENGES

5/17/17

PARTNERS....

In my food truck business, I have a 19-year-old female partner. Yes, I saw so much value in partnering up with her. Yes, I depended a lot on partnering up with her. However, our operation is a major risk because of her attitude. I am the innovator, executer and problem solver of this business. I have responsibilities that I cannot delegate to a person whom I can depend on. And dealing with a teenager is another level of managing. I call it the school of maturism. We have set responsibilities and tasks for each of us. We have agreed on them and signed a contract. But, 25%, her share of the business, "is not enough", she said, because she thinks she is worth more than that. When in reality, her contribution to the business is not worth more. When you know your value and someone undervalues you, madness escalates, and tension clouds the room. You think talking sense would work, but dealing with a teenager is difficult for a business.

6/5/2017

Innovation = knowledge + purpose

Today, while I was riding the bus to my office, one guy talked to his friend about how he lost on this game called Ballot, an app that can be downloaded from the AppStore. I listened, and in my mind, I pictured that guy's future life (not something I would want to be). And I concluded that he has no purpose in life. The lack of innovation and ambition is due to the lack of knowledge and not having a purpose in life. A problem which we are currently facing in our society. "Live your life and survive for the next day" is a mind-killer concept because if that were the case, we would still be riding camels.

These kinds of events encourage me to focus on my goal. A person would say, how do you want me to innovate when the society I live in is a society that lives its present? I read a book called Trigger by Marshall Goldsmith, one of the greatest coaches, and he introduced a story called "Do Not Blame The Empty Boat." The story talks about a merchandiser trying to get from one side of the sea to the other. And a large boat was approaching his boat. He tried to get the attention of the captain by waving and shouting. The large boat hits the merchandiser. The merchandiser barges in anger and frustration since there was no captain in the larger boat. Lesson learned: you decide the fate of your destiny if God permits.

I wanted to share this story of a young man with no purpose because as much as I would be encouraged if I was in an environment that embraced entrepreneurs, I am more fueled to reach my entrepreneurial goal and change the mindset of our community.

The trucking business is going great. In the last two months, we have made more than 130 thousand in revenue. The business is not stable yet; we could have bumps at any time. One of our regular employees, who works in another company, but works part-time with us, was transferred to night duty since his supervisor suspected his tiresome was due to working two jobs. That employee is our cook, who we trained for two months. However, I was lucky that Ramadan is the month of the year when people fast from dawn till dusk. And, our working hours would fit his schedule even after changing duty hours.

After this incident, I put all my force into securing full-time employees to make the business more sustainable. I am also recruiting young and motivated Saudis to work with me. I have picked one so far, and I hope he is up to the challenge.

"Entrepreneurship is the definition of life. You innovate. You feel alive. You live decades to come."

6/9/2017

They decided to Quit!! Though, I know that this will happen sooner or later…

It is Ramadan. We worked for about 4 hours. I have slept for 2 hours since yesterday. The employees were frustrated because the work in Ramadan is usually very challenging as the time is tight between the iftar and fasting time. We usually eat before the morning prayer when we have to start to fast. So to compensate the employees, I offered free burgers for them to eat, but they refused. We waited for a little more time to sell the last burgers. And as I asked to close up the shop and leave, one employee expressed his frustration with a bad attitude and rude behavior. He then started speaking in his language (Filipino).

I could not tolerate wrong behavior, and I got so angry. Although I did not use disrespectful words, I brought up all the good things I have done for them. And I said, "I bought you drinks and lunches, and this is how you repay me." And he responded, "ok, I quit." I was so tired of thinking. I was surprised, even though I expected that this day would come. I did not have much time to think. My mind was just not functioning. I have to find employees with experience who can work with us permanently. Thankfully, because I was working on finding permeant employees, I planned to fly tomorrow to the west of Saudi (Jeddah) to interview two employees. Initially, I wanted to Train the new permanent employees with the part employees who just quit and do not want to continue working with us. Things do not always go in your favor. I was frustrated because I could have controlled my ego, contained the issue, and prevented the part-time employees from quitting.

Our operation has now stopped, and tomorrow I will travel to Jeddah (west of Saudi) to visit a recruiting agency and hopefully find the employees that can help us make the business more sustainable. Although the stoppage hurts the business, I am excited to resolve the challenge. I also started reading a book that my father gifted me on management, "The Five Dysfunctions of a Team." Hopefully, when I read it in the next couple of days, I will better understand why the problem occurred and make sure it is avoided in the future.

"Always expect the worst, and develop a contingency plan"

6/11/2017

One day, I flew to Jeddah, recruited the right employees, and returned to Dammam (the origin of our business). Although it wasn't an easy trip or solution, I feel very proud of how I overcame the problem vigilantly and with confidence in the future success of the food truck business. I have interviewed almost 20 employees, and it wasn't easy to pick the right person for the job. But honestly speaking, I did not settle for the best of the worst. I am confident that I picked the right people for the job with the minimum risk. If they decide not to work with us, the agency will replace them with zero expenses. Although the service cost of this advantage is relatively expensive, it is worth it because the business will suffer tremendously if faced with a similar employee problem.

6/15/17

Operating a food truck business isn't as easy as it sounds. Working inside a food truck is also challenging due to limited space and the need to stand all the time.

When the part-time employees decided to quit working, I thought the salary was a good pay, so why would they mess up such an opportunity. They work 4 to 5 hours and almost double their monthly income. The thought of losing employees hasn't crossed my mind. After I reacted poorly as a leader, I thought I was the reason why they decided to quit. And I started questioning my management style. I even read a book on management/leadership called "The dysfunctions of a team," gifted by my father. I found the book hanging on my shelf. Having suffered from team dysfunction, I was motivated to read the book. I very much recommend it. It explains leadership in a compelling narrative.

After I hired the new employees, I changed my training style. I used a smooth voice with strong and inspiring words. After two days of training, I can tell you that the new hires got hold of the operation pretty quick. They also understood my management style as reasonably straightforward, with no fuss and muss. I can see a huge difference when I compare my current training with the one I used to conduct with previous employees. It took me two weeks to reach a stable operation. Why did it take all that time for a fairly simple job? Two simple reasons – communication and continuous willingness to work. And I concluded that communication with the ex-employees was why I lost them. And I am happy that I have new employees who are fast learners and I can communicate well with them.

**"Communication is the key to strong
Leadership/Management"**

6/29/2017

I hired a Saudi and trained him for a week. Suddenly, his grandfather passed away, and his emotional state did not allow him to continue working with us. And so, I had to look for another qualified Saudi I could depend on to perform his utmost. I did, and he is currently in the training phase. Oh boy, how much time it takes to train an employee until he reaches your expectations (and you won't be satisfied, you will always want more from your employees). I hope he will continue because our operation needs sustainability.

Fortunately, my partner and I diagnosed a future problem that we will face in the future in our operation. The problem is the expiration of the visa of one of the employees in four months. The problem would have put us on the ground if we had not thought ahead. This employee is the sole driver of our food preparation. Of course, the employee is trained by us, but losing her would jeopardize the quality of the food prepared.

To plan forward and mitigate future risks, we have developed a plan to recruit new employees, rent a store to transfer the operations from the kitchen of a house to a stable well-established preparation lab (some people call it the central kitchen, but I call it a lab because on many occasions we have faced many issues that we had no clue of resolving so we were experimenting, whether it's the temperature of the room, storage method, process guidelines, etc..).

This reality is what makes startups vulnerable and always fighting to survive. You have to look forward and detect what could go wrong. For the first year, startups shouldn't be concerned about cost but should focus on quality and marketing.

7/3/2017

As an entrepreneur, I always seek to develop myself and gain more skills to cultivate better results and get closer to the ultimate goal. Unfortunately, I am always in a fight with myself. I want to quit my current job because I am not learning what will get me closer to my passion. However, I need my job to have the ability to live with my own money and be financially capable of making future investments. I am struggling with my time at work, as I could use the 8 hours to deliver better and more valuable results. I am also struggling with my desires as a man and human being. However, how can I pursue my goals and have fun simultaneously? I know I need to balance, but I don't know how to achieve that balance. Balance feels like a myth. I am scared of myself because I am the worst enemy of myself.

7/30/17

Relationships…

Being a food truck owner and a marketer through social media, I meet many people and connect with a lot too. I was sure to build a network with people. However, since all of this is new to me and being an introvert, building those relationships was hard. I believe I have high standards of the people I want to associate with. My experience of traveling and studying abroad for more than eight years has taught me not to waste my time with people who are not better than me. It is much better and healthier to have meaningful relationships.

Food Truck …

After employing the new Saudi, he decided to quit because, as he said, the "work is tiring." Although I was'nt glad that he quit working with us very early, I was happy because I don't like complainers. Another decision I am very proud of is focusing on finding a co-founder on board to assist me in building the business. I have trusted a solid person with a strong personality. This guy is the guy who worked for me at the beginning, who had to leave because of a family member's loss. I convinced him to work with us because I see so much value in him joining our business.

To build a reliable operation with consistent quality, we rented a store and developed a central kitchen to prepare the food. It will increase the cost since the central kitchen needs workforce, electricity, appliances, and rent payments. It is worth it because it will allow us to have a stable operation set to grow.

8/8/2017

After four months of operating a business, I have found a co-founder who is valuable to the business. He was the first person I employed after almost two months of operating the business. He is the guy I employed a while ago who lost his grandfather. I realized how valuable my instincts are in knowing the right person to employ and the added value he can offer. He is the one who was in charge of pushing the municipality to issue the registration for the food truck after a battle of 4 months. I offered him a stake in the profit and allowed him to be in the founder's team.

In the past two months, I had to employ Saudis to cover the same position three times in two months. A high monthly turnover can kill a business from having a stable operation and consistent customer satisfaction. And so, as suggested by Rakan, we created flexible working hours. We decided to offer new employees a three working-day system per week. The system will allow the employee to enjoy the work and not get bored by the routine. Employing gave me a chance to test my temper and preference in what kind of employees I want to hire. I have made mistakes, which forced me to think of what I can do to mitigate bumpy roads. My understanding of people's behavior and intention have improved drastically. And, you will never understand it until you deal with people. Leading is not an easy job; however, managing is not difficult.

In the next phase of the food truck business, we had to build a central kitchen to prepare the food and have stable operations. It took us almost a month to build it. Although it is a must, it will extremely increase our operational cost. What frightens us is that once you increase the cost, you must increase your income. However, we still haven't implemented a way to increase our income. Although we planned to build another truck with the same line of products, I figured why not expand to a different line with the same concept. And so, I contacted an established juicer business called Palma to collaborate and do business together. They were intrigued. Hopefully, we can build something that will explode the market.

10/5/17

After almost a year of grinding and experiencing different kinds of struggle, you start thinking about your goals and if you are close to accomplishing them. You also start thinking about the time you spend every day trying to achieve your four-year goals. I work in the biggest company in Saudi Arabia from 7 am to 4 pm. And the work I am doing doesn't meet my interest. Then I have a two-hour break. Then I am off to operate the food truck till 12 am — no time to invest in myself, whether by reading, attending conferences or networking. You start questioning your decisions and your daily routine if they are healthy and will pay off in the future. It is 1:55 on a Thursday afternoon. I felt bored with a routine job, so I decided to express my thoughts.

I realized that if you set a goal to achieve, you will have to sacrifice another. For instance, my goal is to reach a certain income, and once I do, I will quit my job. However, I am sure that the best investment is investing in yourself because once you do that, everything else will follow – Money, Knowledge, State of mind, Experience, and Happiness. I confess that I currently feel lonely. I want friends to fill that gap. Friends who are going to live up to my standard. And I won't be able to do so if I don't have time. I am unsure if I am blaming the time or rushing on things since it has been six months since we started operating the food truck business. Life is … I thought I already figured out what Life is. I think life should equal satisfaction. But how to achieve that?

**"Life is a Struggle. Is it painful or adventurous?
How you relate to struggles depends on you."**

10/20/2017

When your plate is full of problems, and you are trying to keep the train moving, you start to think of failure and what ifs that could drive you crazy. The main thing is how to make a fuel that drives you to success.

The Co-founder that I picked has left me. The new store that we developed to prepare the food is lacking workforce. I have been looking for almost two months and did not find the right fit. One of my employees expressed work fatigue and asked to leave. I convinced him to stay for a little more time. Also, one of the Saudi employees left. Thankfully, I kept one Saudi applicant hanging just in case something similar happened. I also have government registrations to process and approve.

With little time and many commitments that shackle your business development, you feel like you are running out of oxygen. I want to do other stuff, like being part of an organization and working on new projects. I have one month to resolve all of these issues

**"If you don't have the time, does it mean
you are not managing it well?"**

12/9/2017

Over the past three weeks, many events occurred.

The first event was an intense struggle between my partner and me. As you may know, we depended on my partners' maids to prepare the food until we built our store and had employees solely responsible for the business's preparation side. The store was set up two months ago, and we are still searching for the right employees. We tried to hire different employees, but we were not successful. One talked a lot and performed less; another refused to work in a small enterprise; the last was Hindu and could not work in a beef-oriented restaurant for religious reasons. So for the first month of operating the central kitchen to prepare the food, we still depended on the maids, which was still good until one of the maids had to leave because the family of my partner did not want the maid to continue to work while they pay for her salary. I have offered to pay her. I even offered to pay for the maid's flight change fee. But, no luck. The parents of my partner did not care. The business lost one knee of its operation, but it did not stop us from continuing to work. The maid left, and we participated in an event. My partner did not plan for the event, and I had to step in. Her excuse for being unprepared was invalid. On the first day at the event, we prepared an adequate quantity to sell. On the second and third days, we tripled the quantity. The work of preparing the food was not easy. I worked almost 12 hours a day to fulfil the needs of the business and join forces with the preparation side of the business. It was exhausting and rewarding at the same time because we sold out every day.

However, since I am organized and prefer to plan when my partner is a reactive person, many delays and miscommunication from my partner's end were frustrating. I like things to be close to perfect, especially if it is within our hands. I remember the moment very well. I tried to call my partner at 7 pm while customers were waiting for orders, and the time was ticking. She did not answer (the whole day, she wasn't answering my calls, but she was texting me through WhatsApp), and I sent a text to imply that your miscommunication is disrespectful. She exploded with anger and decided not to work for the next two weeks! I was very irritated. I tried to convince her to keep working. I even asked her to meet and resolve all issues face-to-face. But, she took a firm decision. I knew she was testing me and wanted me to beg her to return. Thankfully, I was so determined that no one would stop me from achieving what I desired, which was the success of the vision of the business. I took responsibility for all of her duties. And, I excelled in them, with minimum problems. During these two weeks, I was immensely thinking of what actions I should take in response to her abandoning the business. I have consulted my parents and a personal coach of mine. I was frustrated since my development plans depended on having a desciplined partner and a success seeker. I was almost ready to break the partnership.

I have set up the store and the truck to work by themselves. However, my vision of the business will be delayed big time. After two weeks, my partner and I met and discussed what went wrong. Although she was furious to blame me for her irrational decision, she sensed her loss of the business. She returned to her senses and apologized profusely for her attitude and for abandoning the business when it needed her the most. She also promised me that it wouldn't happen again in the future. Before her apology, I was ready to present my solution: to accept her back in the business on one contingency; if she repeated her irrational decision, her stake in the business would diminish to 5%. However, her apology made me think of what my father advised me to do, which is to let go and think of her importance in the future of the business. Things are smooth now, and we are back on track with no business issues.

In this situation, I have learned that people need to understand each other by communicating well. I also learned that people would protect their ego and won't realize what they will lose in return (Business, Relationships, Respect, ...)

The next stepping stone event toward the success of the business is developing a second truck. The truck will be structured to our desire and have all the equipment we want. Hopefully, it will be a successful decision, as many government changes are being implemented, like government reforms in regulations and the infrastructure of business operations. VAT is on the way, a new challenge to the business, and it is very early for us to endure as a small enterprise.

"Lack of communication is the main reason for failure."

1/7/2018

A very tough year indeed for all businesses. The year of survival as well as the redistribution of market share. Some businesses will bleed, and others will acquire more customers.

I know that you shouldn't grow your business in your first year, but you should focus on developing your quality with the available tools. I did not follow that because I thought the faster you grow, the faster you can dominate the market. That is especially true for the food truck industry as the concept is fairly new to the Saudi market. It is for sure a promising industry. However, the Saudi economy has a lot of uncertainty. If we see the cost to operate a business, it is very discouraging to open a business today, especially if your business depends on expats. And, as a food truck looking to expand and have a stable operation, we depend on expats. Many other factors are affecting businesses, outlining some of those challenges: the newly introduced VAT and the price increase of energy and car fuel, which drive the massive decrease in purchasing power. Before I started the food truck business, I wanted to use the cash generated to invest it in other businesses, just like the cash cow business concept. Instead, the money generated has been spent to have a stable operation and grow the business. Today we have spent 90 thousand riyals to have a central kitchen, a significant milestone to support the expansion. We have also spent 50 thousand riyals on buying another truck. The truck's purpose is to grow and expand the menu by having a bigger truck.

If I had gone back two months ago, I would have re-spent the money to grow the business. Because at that time, it made sense, and we had the cash to do so. However, I would have stuck to the business basics and not grown in the first year of business.

Although I know the market will go down due to the increased cost of living in Saudi Arabia, it is the best time to get into the market. I say this because I am sure many businesses will close in 2018. Businesses today are seeking survival if it is worth it. Imagine if you are living in a district where twenty food services feed that district, and, in 2018, seven of the restaurants closed. Either that increases the share of the remaining 13 restaurants, or it will be an excellent opportunity for newcomers to dominate the market share of the closed restaurants.

That will surely be the case. And to succeed in this strategy to penetrate the market, you need to understand the change in human behavior driving the market. You need to evaluate your pricing, type of food, and added value of your business.

I learned in this market environment that if you wait for things to get better, you will suffer a lot. However, if you fight to shift how you operate your business, even if it is a marginal change, you are a winner. Raising the white flag or cashing out can also be wise in this market blood bath, which will minimize your losses.

1/8/2018

Working daily in a job and operating a business…

I have been struggling with my consciousness. The consciousness of fear of failure if I quit my job to pursue the desire of being an entrepreneur. Am I willing to give up my lifestyle for the sake of my business? Or am I willing to give up me focusing on one thing for the sake of my lifestyle? Am I willing to learn things I do not desire to use in the future or learn specific things that will help me reach my dream?

The thought of operating a food tuck only, with no assurance of success, which is the case for everything in life, does not give me the courage to dedicate my entire time to the business. Also, after eight months of operating the food truck business, my motivation has dimmed down, which has a lot to do with being an employee in the morning and a business owner in the evening. It is like living two life's in one day. In the morning, you are a refinery engineer. And, in the evening, you are in a food truck serving burgers. No connection whatsoever!

I want to be a full-time entrepreneur and focus on one thing. What will I do in reality? I do not know. I lack the courage to quit and accept that business is a risk and it can succeed or fail. I am also worried that if I quit, I will be more distant from the human interaction I am blessed to have in my day-to-day job.

"Fear is good, but it can kill you too."

1/20/2018

Ever feel like you are not doing enough. Then, you are afraid to take a vacation because that will let your energy go away. That is the side effect of burnout. In my case, I was burnout as well as demotivated. I took a vacation two weeks ago to relax and focus on the business. I also felt that this was the end of my daily job since I thought the growth and expansion would take their course. However, the business climate is very uncertain, and the economy is still making reform changes. I will still hold on to my job until things are clear and the future business direction becomes clearer. I believe that operating a business in this continuously changing market is the best experience an entrepreneur can have because there are challenges every step forward that require the entrepreneur's immediate response. It makes you an expert in problem-solving.

I feel demotivated to get back to work in the morning and manage my business in the evening. I feel like my body and mind have suffered enough. My mind is exploding with thoughts of failure and regret. If I had a good relationship with entrepreneurs, I would have quit long ago. However, since I am an introvert, I want to have a small circle of friends. It is not about time but the quality of friends I am looking for. And that is backfiring because I feel like I am running alone in the woods. I optimistic that I will feel better and find the friends I am looking for.

Focus is the drive of your energy. And, trying to multi-task is not helping me to be at my full best. I need to focus on one goal. Read a book called "The ONE THING." It talked about focusing on one thing at a time. The book goes through strategies that you can use to get things done with energy balance (willpower) and minimum effort. So, I pursued the book's advice and started writing a list of actions I needed to complete every day. I start my day with the most crucial action, which needs my full attention and energy. I can go through the other items when I finish my top-of-the-list items. I try to keep my list short and distribute the items for more than one day. Imagine if you do only one important item every day. What is the outcome? Extreme efficiency and unprecedented achievements. Multitasking is a myth of excellence. And, it is never the right strategy to do business. If you focus on one thing and leave all other distractions like your phone, email, thoughts, etc... you will get more things done. One example in the book is Apple and how Jobs focused on developing the ONE PRODUCT instead of having many average products.

I hope my decision to continue working in the day-to-day job is the right decision.

"Multitasking is not the game. Focus is the Game"

Willpower

I know what I wish to accomplish. I also know that it is not an easy road. It won't be easy to be a successful person. It is a bumpy road full of surprises.

I am also a worrier, and doubts sometimes cloud my judgments. Am I taking the right decision? Will sacrificing the experience of my daily job to accomplish my desires have a more significant impact on my future? Or will I fail and wish that I had taken a different decision? I know that failure is a learning experience.

I realized that willpower is the driver of your hustle, creativity, and, hopefully, success. The question is, how do you gas up your willpower daily? How can you be at the top of your game every day? Willpower is a phycological effect; your mind thinks with what you feed it. Your mind is like a plant; and it gows once it is fed with water. "you cultivate what you feed your mind with," and that is how your willpower can be powered up. It is easier said than done because it requires a massive open-mindedness and effort to discard the physical and mental pain. If you are not feeling pain, you are not gaining anything. It is all about mindset and how you can understand what your mind is being fed for better results and continuous willpower.

"Willpower is like a plant. It needs to be fed with great thoughts to cultivate its fruits."

1/28/2018

Truck Number 2 has been executed. In less than one month and the truck will be ready for business. 100,000 is spent on this project, without considering the operational cost, which I estimated to be 35,000. Do we have that money in the bank? No.

The main hassle in operating a business is the workforce. You want to operate your business at the minimum cost. However, it is always not the case, especially in the food industry, since you have a high turnover. And the risk of expansion relies on having a skilled workforce to maintain the food quality. The business lives on its edge; every penny saved is drained through expansion. We are living in a high-risk situation. However, I remember how Philip knight managed his cash flow when developing Nike. He did not save a penny and dumped all his cash into more inventory and expansion, although he was in debt and was almost going to jail at some point. I am not copying his model, but I am replicating his drive in business and his passion for getting the business out of its suffering. I do not know if the plan will work, but I believe we are on the right path.

Before, I feared the economy would kick us out of the game. However, when evaluating the expansion of the business, I looked at it from two sides. First, the business is currently small, and that does not motivate me to wake up the following day, so I needed to do something bigger than myself. Second, expanding will bring great value to the business, such as expanding our customer base, having more robust sales, achieving business freedom, and developing a better operation, which are the success factors of a business. One thing I want to elaborate on is business freedom. It is the freedom from looking after your back from duplicates and competition. I accepted the competition, but I had to do all I could to drive away the competition legally. However, by expanding, your business brand will roar like a lion in your industry, especially if you know how to use it to your advantage. And, the name of your competition will fade because they are not seen in the public eye as a strong business.

"What motivates you to wake up the next morning?"

3/16/18

I just took a vacation leave for about a month from my day-to-day job to concentrate on the food truck business, as the second food truck is ready to open its doors for customers. I have been planning for this day for more than five months. The planning included training employees, deploying new products, branding, and strategizing to acquire new customers. Every penny saved has been poured into expansion and setting a more substantial business. It is time for branding and anchoring our name for everyone to know. We have worked hard the last year to fix our mistakes quickly and avoid repeating them. We have also developed a stiffer skin towards challenges, as we faced partnership disagreements, boycotting, high turnover rate, regulation changes, maintenance problems, you name it. Looking back to one year of operation, it sounds like a dream. I cannot believe that we survived. The business is growing, and the challenges are on a bigger scale that requires a focused and vigilant operation. I feel the pressure as well as the excitement of expansion. I remember saying that the business used to be fragile initially, but now it is stable and can handle bigger obstacles.

With all the economic reforms and changes in regulations, I thought the business would be affected drastically. Think about it; the economy is at its worst, and most businesses in all industries suffer from low revenue. The labor force is applying stricter regulations that are eating away business profits. Many would say that today is the worst day to open a business when our food truck is expanding. I thought the slow in purchasing power would hit our food truck revenue. When I realized that money would be flowing even if the market is down, the innovative business is the one that understands what the customer wants. The real business mind would see a down market as an opportunity, these times are when many businesses will vanish, and many successful new ones will flourish.

One lesson I learned, which took me a long time to accept, is that all businesses/organisations depend on dealing with people. A former CEO of Boeing stated in an interview when asked what made your management successful, "it is all about the people." I thought about it and realized that in the last year of leading the food truck business, I wanted people who would be comfortable with me when I should be looking for talented and passionate people. The same concept applies to my business partner; I thought she was causing a problem because she did not have the same mindset I have and neglected her experience in the food industry and her strong role in the business's success. She is talented but lacks a professional mindset, and it is my job as a leader "people's person" to understand her and guide her thoughts to focus on the benefits of the business. I found that this has cleared my heart and made me more focused on reaching the vision of the food truck business.

"A leader is a people's person."

3/21/18

A disaster… or shall I call it, god's call.

The first day of operating the new truck had a lot of events. I drove since 7 am, trying to fix what needed to be fixed and prepare the truck for the opening day. At about 4 pm, employees were late and hadn't yet started preparing the truck. One hour later, the employees realized they had forgotten to bring many important supplies, and they had me driving around the city to purchase them. It was like a marathon, trying to drive around and not be late for the opening time. I secured mostly everything and arrived at the truck at 7:45 pm; then, I saw the gas leaking. I was about to have a heart attack since any ignition source would have exploded the investment of 6 months of work and money.

Time passed. We started taking orders. We started smelling something unusual. It was coming from the grill. I asked the cook if he had cleaned the grill and prepared it to grill food on since it is a new equipment. He did not. And, we stopped taking orders for 30mins to fix this issue. Then we resumed taking orders. Since I advertised the opening pretty well, we had a full house. 40 mins passed, and another kind of smell filled the truck. It smelled like fire. I walked out of the truck and saw a cloud of huge smoke and a huge hot spot on the exterior. It turns out that the truck was on fire. We had to take action immediately, close everything down, and shut down any energy source. We took the gas far away from the truck and called the fire department. We saw fire, and some of the customers were kind enough to help us and offered us their fire extinguishers to be sprayed on the fire source. The firefighters arrived and put the fire down.

Now, when this happened, I was not surprised. I was somewhat depressed, but I felt like it was normal. I knew that sometimes we don't get what we wish and desire. I was more frustrated about how I would repair the damage from the fire. I will send it back to the manufacturer since the guarantee will cover all the damages. That is how I felt emotionally.

What helped me the most was my tendency to think logically and discard discouraging thoughts.

From a business owner's perspective, I lost a lot of money. I have an asset that is draining money. And, my overhead cost is high since I am over-employed. As discussed with the manufacturer, the damage won't take more than two days. And, it will hopefully be fixed and ready to generate money.

When the manufacturer opened the truck walls to fix the damage, they found that the electric cable caught on fire due to being exposed to high heat from the fryer. After I knew, my thoughts shifted labeling what had happened from a disaster to a blessing. Because the cables getting on fire could have turned the whole truck into ashes. They were able to fix the truck and return it to us in no time.

**"At all circumstances, think of what can be
done and not what could have been done."**

3/30/2018

Perspective!!

When you are in school, your expectations can be measured. If you succeed in a test, you will get a percentage for your achievement. Above 90% means you are doing excellent, while above 80% means good. Does life work that way?

When I graduated from High school, I did not know what I should pursue. I just knew that I was destined to accomplish something great. I did not know how to assess what I was doing on a percentage basis to achieve self-satisfaction, to know that I was on the right track. Life hits you with many mysteries and codes you need to unpuzzle. I remember going to my supervisor at work, and I asked him, "how can I get an "S" (significant) at my employee performance," which is the best performance an employee could get. And he replied, "Do not think of it this way. Just do your best at whatever you are doing." And I was frustrated a little because I did not know what it meant at the time as a fresh graduate. Work performance can be measured, but your performance is complicated. If you think about it, failure in an exam means you must retake the course, while failure in life's work means achievement, experience and lessons for the future. That means you are gaining more than losing.

4/1/2018

Expectations…

If we see the successful beginnings of business leaders, their age varies. Garry Vee started his multi-million marketing company in his thirties. After ten years of starting Walmart, Sam Walton hit his first million in revenue at age 54. Ortega founded ZARA at the age of 39. And many other examples who have started their success at different ages.

I think I am worried if the train of success passes by me without honking. I am afraid that one day I will sit and regret some decisions that I have taken and compare my status with my friends and see that they are way ahead of me. Are my fears healthy? I know they are not and will over-stress my mind and depletes my energy. Do I know how to deal with this feeling? I know that if I am 30, I can be the next Reid Hoffman (Founder of LinkedIn), and at 50, I can build the next MacDonald's (Ray Kroc founded MacDonald's in his 50s).

"Expectations cannot be measured.
Expectations mean realising what you can be
with what you are doing today."

4/6/2018

With all the planning…you will face failure

Since I was planning to execute the second truck, I recruited an employee to be a cook. I have trained him for two months. I also taught him the values that we stand for as a business. It takes a lot of effort and time to prepare and train an employee to fit your standards. Although I created a system for new hires to dive in immediately, be productive and understand their responsibility, it is not enough to produce quality work. And that is very critical when you have a reputation to preserve.

The newly recruited employee felt sick and expressed his suffering. As a consequence, the employee was excused from work to rest. I then sat with him to understand his condition. The employee expressed that he had been suffering from breathing problems for ten months since his arrival to Saudi Arabia, and his condition has worsened every month. His body looked pale and weak. I took him to the hospital, and the doctor did his routine check-up. The doctor says his health is fine. The next day, the employee's condition worsened, and I took him to 3 different hospitals. We did x-rays and blood tests and went to a Cardiologist and Otolaryngologist specialists. Both specialists expressed no concern. The doctors pointed to me that the employee might be suffering from depression. And his mental condition of depression is making up his health problems.

All that means is that the employee is lying to himself. How will you convince this guy, whose education is limited, that his mind makes up his condition? It is hard as hell. I thought if I asked the doctor to talk to him about his condition, he would understand and get out of that mental block. But, I knew that it would take a long time for him to change his thoughts from a sick mindset to the strong, healthy one. The next day after visiting three different hospitals, his health deteriorated because he wasn't eating well. If you have seen the employee, you would think he is dying, even though he is only 24. I was so frustrated because I could not change his mindset. I was also more frustrated to have wasted months training him.

Losing that employee meant that one leg of our operation was down. Plan.. plan.. plan.. and plan to fail. Failure after planning is a probability. But, without planning, you will fail. However, with proper planning, you minimize the risk of failing big. Once you realize that nothing is a flat line or a straight incline, you will be prepared to face the worst.

On the same day the employee left, another employee replaced him without interrupting our operation. I planned for the day when that same cook could not continue to work with us to be ready for his replacement.

"Plan to succeed, and plan to fail."

4/7/2018

How Can you create a system that will develop itself? In other words, how can you take your hands off the business and have it work on its own, independently?

The food truck has two main operating segments; preparation and cooking.

Preparation: there are three main responsibilities for the preparation side — grounding & cutting, cleaning and preparing all the needed supplies for the cooking part of the operation. And for each responsibility, an employee must follow a system to simplify the process and eliminate human mistakes.

Cooking: Getting the supplies inside the truck, cooking the food, and cleaning. And for each of these responsibilities, a system was developed to maintain the quality.

Now with all the developed systems, employees make mistakes that shouldn't be made since there are systems that assist them in having a smooth operation. Having mistakes means the system is not being followed. However, I have done incentives and an accountability system to encourage compliance and productivity. Mistakes are still present. What is the main reason? Lack of supervision. Employees will try to neglect and bypass systems without continuous supervision at every operation step. Every employee's work needs to be assessed and supervised to ensure that the employee is doing quality work and following the systems.

When we create systems, we think that the employee is fully responsible for performing the job at the utmost quality. However, in reality, employees will always try to minimize the headache of work, even when simplified. The only solution to drive your operation into continuity and stability is to create another supervision system. That is why big cooperates have many departments and many divisions within. It is so that other departments/divisions push every department/division to be productive and perform quality work.

> **"A system shall always be supervised
> and assessed by other systems."**

4/8/2018

A coup with changes and developments

Especially in the food industry that deals with the customer directly (B2C), changes are pretty fast. Many things could drive change. The opening of a new restaurant (competition), supply shortage, customer buying power, customer behavior, market stresses… The idea is how can you turn those changes to your advantage? If the world moves fast, you need to move faster. This principle applies to all businesses.

Another thing that needs to be considered is your added value. No matter what the factors are, your added value is what you should build on. If you neglect to differentiate your business, whether in your product, service or experience, concentrate on it, sustain its success and improve it. MARKETING is the big game; if you have an added value, it will market itself. But, it won't market itself forever. In today's world, the combination of added value and marketing dominates any market. People will forget you in seconds if you do not market your product. Marketing does not mean advertising only; it means continuously reminding your customer about your product in a way that sticks in their mind. If I see our product, I know that the added value is the sauce because I observe the customer's reaction when he tastes the sauce. I listen to the customer when he asks about the sauce and how they had been craving it for a week or dreaming about it while asleep.

Though we focused on word of mouth, we did spend some of our money on social media marketing, customer experience, charities, and events. And, in my opinion, its impact is continuous for our customers compared to using influencers and traditional advertisement, which I call lazy marketing. Real smart marketing is the marketing that lets your employees fight for you even when you are not available. And that can be accomplished by being innovative at your marketing and by marketing a story, not a statement.

In my experience, the best marketing strategy is giving customers an experience, especially in the food industry. Customers usually are fed up with the regular treatment they are getting everywhere. See Starbucks, for example; a great cup of coffee only does not bring the customer back the next day to wait in line. It is the special treatment and recognition of the customer that he is valuable, while providing a great product. I believe that customer experience Marketing is the best in today's world. Experience marketing, be it in the form of a video, image, entertainment, service, smart promotions and many other forms.

CHAPTER 4

PARTNESHIP FALLOUT

5/11/2018

You think you have mastered partnership, but the partnership is far from perfect. A partnership is a sacrificing game plan. Every partner thinks his role will stay as agreed from day one, but everything changes daily in business, especially if your ambitions are high.

In the past month or so, tension escalated due to the demanding business needs. The partner expressed that her input into the business has exceeded the limits of her capabilities through text messages. The partner also refused to conduct a business meeting face to face. The partner also excluded herself from product development responsibility when previously agreed upon. If something was to be out of control in the central kitchen (the partner's main responsibility, as indicated in the partnership contract), the partner would not be dependable to fix it.

As the leader of this small enterprise, it is imperative to take decisions - either I set solid partnership grounds with severe consequences or break up the partnership. This is a decision that I will leave for my partner to make.

I realized that partnership is like a house. If not built on solid foundations, it will collapse. When I recalled the partnership signing date, it would have been a disaster if we hadn't covered many aspects of the partnership agreement. My business partner, who has minimal business experience, would ruin the partnership because she thought 25% was not enough. And, I was naïve to think that partnership would be stronger than greed. However, the partner wanted more equity in the business which she had mentioned when we started operating business, but I neglected. Every word and thought that come from your partner must be accounted for. If you neglect it, it will come back to you in the future.

The things I missed to include in the partnership contract are financial responsibility, development, marketing, supervision responsibilities, communication mediums, profits distribution, and future roles of partners that will be determined during business growth. These responsibilities must be in detail. For example, communications must be conducted face to face weekly. And the partners will be held accountable if the agreement is not complied with. Partners also need to know that they will be employees under their leader if they ever decide to work in the business. The same must be applied to all the other areas to ensure all partners understand what they are getting into.

> **"Partnership is like a house. if it is not built on solid grounds, it will collapse."**

6/29/2018

Breaking partnerships are brutal for your business and psychological health. I remember continuously thinking of my decision and whether I have done the right thing. I was counting the money that would be lost and the effort spent in this business that might be wasted. A year of the partnership will be shredded, and its value will diminish. However, whenever I thought of the partnership values, I asked myself, how the team would function when the business is expanding rapidly; it did not seem that our partnership would be successful. Will she be vigilant 95% of the time when the business is big and generates a lot of revenue? Will she put business success before personal interests? Whenever I ask these questions, I realize that my partner's attitude and fluctuating productivity cannot benefit the business.

I consulted three lawyers during the partnership breakdown to end the contractual agreement. It was very insightful and gave me a perspective of the law system from three different angles. I found the person who did "free" consultations to lore you to his nest. Although it was valuable to listen to different perspectives, they were not competent enough to assure me of excellent results.

The lawyer, who had written the initial partnership contract, developed the contract with many clauses that contradicted its own and did not represent the true partnership. When the partnership was deemed to end, I came to their office and asked for their services. The lawyer was trying to oppress me and explained that they would act in the interest of both parties in the contract and will not in any way be working for me. And, I broke the news to the arrogant lawyer of his poor contract and ambiguous terms. The lawyer was speechless. One minute he was accused of orchestrating a fraud agreement; the other minute, he was apologizing.

I approached another lawyer who is one of my father's friends. He is very competent and works for a big law firm in the country. He is the kind of lawyer you would want to get if you are at the executive level. He is a great lawyer and a very understanding and logical person. He knows the system very well and is an expert in his profession. But his services are costly; believe me, it is worth it. A valuable lawyer creates a shield for the rest of your life. And knowing that I would be working with a strong lawyer meant the partnership would be put to bed for good.

When I say breaking a contractual agreement is brutal, I mean it. When we set terms for breaking the partnership, the partner expressed the unfairness of the terms and thought she deserved more than her right to get. I remember the day after I gave her two choices (either stay with penalty of 5% reduction in equity if the same business attitude continues or break the partnership). She came to the store and took everything she owned, even the measuring spoon and all the work procedures of the store's operation, which is really immature. I sensed something of a kind might happen, so I took all precautions for a smooth operation. Though the employees were uncomfortable and felt threatened by her actions, I had to set a meeting with the whole team to assure them of their value to the business.

Agreeing on terms to end the partnership was like a needle in a haystack. One day, the partner agrees; another day, the partner disagrees. I even gave up on my terms just to end this toxic partnership, but I had no luck. After seeing that all roads to agreeable terms were closing and the continuous threats I received from the partner, I reached out to my father's associate/friend, who was very welcoming. And he agreed to take my case and end the partnership.

"Always ask for the perspective of more than one party when acquiring consultations."

7/13/18

This old man who lives close to the food truck is a retired soldier. When we started operating the food truck in the garden, the old man came to our food truck with his car and tried to intimidate us. He asked us to leave and look for another location and threatened to call the police if we decided to stay. Though we had so many neighbors who lived close by, the only person who did not like our presence was the retired old man.

During our food truck operation, we faced many issues enforced by the old man's hate. He used to call the municipality hotline and raised false complaints. One of his complaints was that our customers blocked his house while the customers were eating in their cars, and when the municipality received any complaints, they had to act and resolve the complaint. But, we were always ready for the inspectors who came to check the validity of the old man's complaints. The old man did not stop by just calling the hotline; he went to the municipality director and raised formal complaints to kick our food truck out of our location, though the location was fully approved by the municipality guidelines. When the old man did not see that the municipality heard his complaints, he went to the city emirate to raise safety complaints. It distracted our operation, as these false complaints kept pounding at us from every angle. After he raised a complaint in the emirate, the complaints were taken very seriously, eventhough they were false complaints. The emirate then sent a letter to the municipality to remove our food truck from the location, and the municipality acted upon the emirate's request and sent a task force to stop our food truck. It was a devastating moment to see the municipality task force asking us to stop our food truck like we were criminals. I saw the old man coming from his house with a big smile on his forehead like he had won. I spoke to him at the front door of his house. I told him, when is this hate going to stop? When are you going to realize that we are not doing anything wrong and accept that we are not abusing the system like you are? His reaction was somewhat expected. He said, "I will not rest until I do not see your truck anymore."

We did stop the food truck for a couple of days until we showed the municipality our registration and that we were operating our food truck legally. I then went to the emirate to understand the old man's claims and resolve the issue. We sent a letter to the emirate explaining our stand and how we are not affecting the neighbor by operating our business legally. We showed the emirate that the old man's false claims come out of hate and nothing more.

Another issue had presented itself In the past two months due to the old man's non-stop claims. We have been trying to renew the municipality permit for the main food truck. And it turns out that this guy who lives 80 meters away from the truck has raised many complaints throughout the year, requesting the municipality to relocate the food truck away from where he lives. The complaints stated that the house owner is suffering from food smell, and groups are gathering in front of his house. The food truck is near a garden on a congested commercial street, which includes many restaurants and retailers. And we have been going back and forth with the municipality to justify our case and explain that the complaints are invalid. We have also backed our case with photos to assure the municipality of our compliance with the municipality regulations and health standards. The municipality director's mistake is that he put himself in the house owner's shoes, "what if I lived there?" And forgot to stick to the rules and regulations of the municipality. Our case was also supported by the governor, who sent a letter to the municipality requesting them to renew our permit.

The director decided to be on the house owner's side and declined to renew our permit. It was somewhat expected, even though we presented a solid case and factual evidence that the complaints were invalid. These people are entrusted to make the decisions that should help the community , when the municipality director has taken a position that could kill a business helping the community and hiring local citizens. Which was frustrating, especially at a time were unemployment rate was 12.7%.

However, I did not give up. I made a presentation that included videos of the truck location, pictures of the product we sell, how we prepare the food, and how we take care of the public place we operate. I then presented it to the governor of all municipalities. I explained to him our stand and desire to continue working in the exact location where our permit renewal was rejected. Although he did not give me an answer to whether he agreed with us or not, I felt like I won the case because the evidence that I presented was taken positively.

Currently, I have two pending break or make challenges. Partnership breakdown and permit rejection. How can I grow the business when I have very tough issues? I will be honest; psychologically, I am challenged. I built a business to make profits. However, each one of these turning points could force us to go out of business.

**"Dream Big. Dream of winning.
And, always, plan for the risks."**

7/23/2018

I might be discouraging in today's memo, but this will prepare you to face the real challenges in a business. It has been fiften months since I started the food truck business. And the past two months have been the most challenging - ending the partnership, the municipality refused to renew the permit, and saudization and new legislations. Things just burst at once. Instead of thinking of development and systemizing operation, I am focused on resolving issues. I am also worried that I might lose my investment; I am afraid that the years of hustling and growing the business could vanish without a return on investment.

So, I summarized the mistakes that I have made for you to consider when starting a business:

1. You shall start with the government rules and regulations of your business industry you are getting yourself into

    Although even if your business meets the industry legislations, there is a chance of changes that could oppose your strategy. In our case, the food truck regulations were unclear, and many changes were implemented to minimize the number of entrants to the market. We have met all of them and still face problems due to bureaucracies. The most important thing that no one can stop you from building the business is knowing all the regulations that the industry requires. From getting the municipality permits, commerce registrations, labor licenses, etc...

2. Make sure you get in bed with the right people. You must partner with someone willing to run the extra mile for the business.

    The right partner plays a significant role in the success of a business. After going through a brutal partnership breakup, I learned I could have avoided it from the beginning. You will not get what I mean until you go through it. I say that because I have read books and consulted people in business partnerships, but I would not understand it without going through that brutal partnership.

3. Do not overlook points 1 and 2:

    I was aware of many regulations before starting the business. I neglected their future impact and decided to deal with it when it became a problem. It is not a problem as long as it is not currently affecting my operations and I am making profits. But I was wrong. A problem does not disappear unless you do something about it. So if your business industry requires a percentage of citizens to be employed in your business, then meet it and do not bypass it. Sometimes it feels like an ant passing by when an ant means a colony about to coup. Problems will still be problems unless you do something about them.

If I described my feelings today, after all the time and money invested to generate profits, I would sum it into one word, frustration. When you carry the burden of success, you try to avoid issues, and if you do face issues, you want them to be related to operations, management, marketing, and growth, but not governmental issues. I do not know if the business will survive, but I am pushing as hardas I can to overcome those challenges. I am negotiating, talking to government officials, and doing my best to survive. I only ask for one year in business to recover my losses and make a little profit.

"Chase your dream wisely. And, do not spend your money or anyone's money without studying all the aspects of your business."

7/30/2018

Growth…

Isn't that what we all strive for (except for age). We want to know the formula as if it is a fixed reaction. You add A to B, and the result is successful growth. Every person wants to grow something, whether it is a relationship, business, assets, personal value, or savings … However, we do not know how to guide ourselves or businesses in a structured way where we can measure our performance. And, on many occasions, challenges interrupt, resulting in fear and smartness.

Although, in my case, due to partnership issues, government procedures, and bureaucracies, growth is a death wish, I have read a book on growing your business by Royston (Built to Grow?)

Royston asks four questions that would guide you to accelerated and sustainable growth.

1. How to increase the number of customers? (A)
2. How to increase the order value? (M)
3. How to increase the frequency of order? (M)
4. How to increase the retention of customers? (R)

The AMR strategy is to attract, maximize, and retain. In his book, he explains how businesses always think that attraction is the best growth method — attracting new customers, whether by opening more stores or expanding your reach to new customers, which is not the right approach. Typically, businesses lose 10% of customers, which is a great value. Royston explains that it is essential to retain your customers as they are your most valuable asset and contribute more than just sales. They can be your marketing agent (word of mouth), maximizing the order value and frequency of order. This can only be achieved if your business develops the right tools to retain those customers.

One example that stuck in my mind is that of a fine dining restaurant. Once the customer reaches the restaurant, they greet him with his name. They then tell the customer, "we have reserved your usual table," and as they walk the customer through their table. They ask them if they want to start with their usual drink, which boosts the customer's ego because they feel special. Will they be loyal to that restaurant? Definitely! They will even recommend the restaurant to their friends and family. It is an intelligent strategy and takes marginal effort to implement. How much does is its cost? Nothing. They attract more customers, maximize the frequency of orders, maximize the order value, and increase customer retention.

"Your current customers are your most valuable assets."

11/4/2018

The Partners Meeting

Before accepting to meet, I knew that meeting the partner would not add value to the table as I have provided them with formal documents detailing the company's accounting history and suggested that the partnership termination terms have gone back and forth for almost five months.

We scheduled a meeting on a specific day. Although, I came to know that all the discussion points would rotate around my integrity. Because I am no accountant, and the numbers speak for themselves. I entered the meeting room and found my partner and her brother sitting, anxious to fire questions. I started conversing with their lawyer to ease the tension and make an impression. We started the discussion, and one of the questions I received during that discussion was, "why did the forecasted daily targets differ on so many days during the partnership?" Part of the operation strategy was that I set a daily target of how many burgers we should prepare to minimize waste. Although the targets differed marginally, I was shocked and almost laughed at the question because I felt pity to accept such a meeting of interrogation. My answer was, "do you know that the weather forecasted that there is a 90% chance it will rain today?" And the weather was clear as a sky. Then, the opponents burst with anger and started to rumble.

Throughout the discussion, I focused on their lawyer more than trying to convince them of my integrity. And, I learned that lawyers play the role of a judge in tables of case discussion. They make their assumptions and impressions of the people involved in the matter. And that is why I made sure to impress their lawyer, as I knew that the opponent spoke ill of me and described the wrong picture of our partnership. Although I did not speak ill of my partner with my lawyer, I knew that even my lawyer had some doubts. That meeting with the opponent was like the feeling of pitching a business idea to sharks. If I fail to convince them, they will eat the pie themselves.

We discussed the terms, and they were greedy and proposed false presumptions of how much profits we made. I let down my ego and sacrificed to increase their compensation to terminate the partnership for good.

CHAPTER 5

EMPLOYEES AND BUSINESS ACUMAN

11/27/2018

I was spending the weekend at my parents' house in Riyadh, which is 4 hrs drive from Dammam, where I live. Enjoying the day with my family, I received a call to be informed that one of the employees was refusing to work due to personal issues with one of his colleagues and that he had raised a knife threatening to kill him. I was devastated because I was supposed to enjoy the day with my family. However, after hearing the news, I rushed to drive to Dammam. Once I arrived, I met the frightened employee and listened to his story and the personal issue they had with each other. I was upset due to the silly personal issue between the employees that drove them to fight. However, I felt a little at ease because the decision to resolve the conflict between the two employees was easy to take.

The next day, I met with both employees to give each one a chance and clear up the story. One employee has worked with us for two years (JP), and the other for five months (Don). JP was very stubborn and thought that he was the one with authority to decide on that matter. He said he would not apologize for threatening Don and could not work with him. He even stated that Don would be killed if he had to work with him. I tried to talk some sense in JP's mind and remind him of his sick mother waiting for the wire transfer to buy medicine and his unemployed sisters. No progress achieved, he said, "it's either Don or me." I had to pick Don because JP breached the values of the business. He will not apologize to make things right and did not show any guarantees that he will never do it again. I was disappointed to let him go because two years of devotion, loyalty, and hard work contributed to the business's success. I decided to let JP go because we cannot allow that behavior in our business. I also made amendments to hire another employee who can immediately take his role.

3/21/19

Six months ago, I started looking for opportunities outside the F&B market. Opportunities will be sustainable, contribute to the local economy, and have a promising future.

One of the business ideas that I explored is agriculture. Currently, most farms use traditional ways of farming (soil & water), including a tremendous amount of water resources produced in Saudi Arabia (more than 80%). Due to weather issues and many other factors, they have not fulfilled the local market needs. However, since water resources in Saudi are scarce, farming technologies like aquaponics and hydroponics are now more promising. These technologies somewhat eliminate the risk of weather changes since these farms offer controlled environments. I also evaluated broilers since it is a business opportunity in the agriculture industry due to a massive shortage in the current local production. After a thorough data evaluation and speaking to multiple consultants and government representatives, the risks were high, and the game players were big corporations. However, I learned that the main success factor in the agriculture business is marketing. So it does not matter how much you produce; it is how much production you can market/sell.

I then jumped into manufacturing. Saudi imports more than 80% of the manufactured products from clothes, plastics, cars, etc.... Manufacturing is a blue ocean market. Opportunities in the manufacturing industry are tremendous, and the government is investing a huge sum of money to support SMEs and enable them to start their manufacturing businesses. I have met more than one consultant to discuss opportunities with high NPV, and the raw material resources are available in Saudi Arabia. I have found a consulting firm that partnered with the city chamber of commerce, which proved the consultant's strong competency. We conducted a meeting and agreed on a path forward after back and forth negotiations. Although at that time, I took the risk of paying a premium after discussing the deal with more than one person I trusted. The business idea seems to lose its value with time and patience for results. At some point, even if the manufacturing idea is futuristic, you could hit a wall due to demotivating economical environments. I am committed to taking the manufacturing road; however, I am still focusing on the main business (food truck). My thoughts are: since I succeeded in the F&B, why don't I continue expanding in that sector? Because I think the F&B is a rapidly changing business sector, your business has to change fast and coop with the trend.

**"Business success includes some luck.
However, I believe the mindset is what drives success."**

5/14/2019

Jumping from one idea to the other is not healthy…

My father's friend approached me with a business idea I had put to sleep, "Vertical Farming." Although I studied the market and looked into the agriculture market and found that the competition won't be healthy, I decided to give it another look and see if the idea is feasible. What motivated me to look into vertical farming again is the backing I would get from strong investors if the idea turns out to be attractive.

I got excited once I was approached. I felt a flashback of how I felt when I first started to understand the fascinating technologies used in the agriculture business that is rarely being utilized in Saudi Arabia and the advantage that could be achieved by conserving the most important resource, water. I felt like this is the business that will allow me to quit my job and have the ability to pursue business as a full-time job. These were the initial thoughts.

I put everything else (manufacturing) on hold, and I started digging into agriculture again, extracting import reports, meeting vertical farm companies, and talking with friends. I started to remember my thoughts once I visited the Ministry of Agriculture and talked with government representatives. My excitement clouded my judgment, as I felt happy when imagining the vertical farm success. I started to answer opposing questions with discipline and motivation as the drivers for the success of the vertical farm. However, deep in my mind, I knew that vertical farms could not compete in the market because their cost of production is very high compared to traditional farming if you account for the overhead cost. The ministry of agriculture did not incentivize vertical farms in any way.

Another reason is when I compared losing money in a manufacturing business and agriculture industry. Knowing that I have a competitive advantage in the Saudi and international markets and being a manufacturer in a specific product along with a couple of companies is a far better bet than competing with 100+ farms in Saudi Arabia.

Life is about choices, and we are continually bombarded by people trying to propose ideas. Follow your guts, but then you have to question them reasonably with data.

5/15/19

Misjudgments…

Understanding human psychology has been a fascinating reality, as it has helped me understand the people around me and be a better leader. I found that in life, humans continuously encounter a situation and make a wrong decision because they took their feelings midlead them. And that is why you will always have that wealth gap between the poor and rich and disparity in lifestyle. I will outline some misjudgments humans make, which were discussed in the book "Wisdom: from Darwin To Munger."

1. Past Experience

    An experiment was conducted in which a cat was put in a room next to a couple of stoves. And once the cat steps onto the hot stove, it screams and jumps away from the stove. The cat then encounters another cold stove but does not try to step on it. Because the cat's experience of pain due to stepping on the hot stove marked an experience of fear of stepping on stoves.

    In life, we encounter challenges, opportunities, and life decisions. And, because of our past experiences, we tend to make decisions based on how we felt in our past experiences. We then misjudge the situation because not all stoves are hut and miss on opportunities that could have been worthwhile. I am sure you have encountered a person who dislikes a specific cuisine no matter how many stars the restaurant has. And, we feel sorry for them because they miss out on the cuisine. But, if we dig deeper, an experience would be the answer to our mystery.

"Do not miss out, but do not rush to conclusions."

2. Optimism

A fascinating psychological phenomenon. Humans usually think that if they succeeded before, they would succeed again, forgetting how they succeeded in the first place. Due to our previous success, our confidence gets hyped, and we make decisions that are overwhelmed by our optimism. Optimism is a good thing for our minds and health. However, a little overdose of optimism when making decisions could be very painful.

"Monitor your optimism, especially when making decisions, and question them to control the outcome."

3. Do-Something Syndrome

Due to pressure, boredom, failure, and the feeling of no accomplishment, we make decisions that harm us more than pleases us. Making decisions must be based on desire and thorough analysis.

"Do something you know you want and will fight for."

4. Impatience

Humans are short-term thinkers. When we are given a choice to take $10 now or $13 next week, we will most probably pick the $10 option. However, when the options change from $10 six weeks from now or $15 after seven weeks, we will have no problem waiting for one more week to gain more since the wait for a longer <u>Senior Strategic Planning and PMO Professional</u> period seems reasonable. Impatience interferes with what stock we pick, the job we accept, the business we invest in, and so on. Short-term thinkers survive for the short term.

I have suffered from impatience at many turning points in my life. However, my awareness of the misjudgment prepares me to question decisions, take a step back, and think more logically.

"When we ask why, we shall be logical and not emotional."

5/18/19

Employees…

A long-lasting struggle. In the food industry, high turnover is expected. Although our current Saudi workforce has stayed with us for more than a year, hiring a new employee has been challenging lately. As I have been searching for a replacement, more than fifteen people have applied for the job, and I have interviewed eight already. I was shocked by the quality of the interviews.

My style in the interview is not to express power or authority. I have a conversation with the interviewee, and I try to talk about stuff that somewhat relates to his life. I then go into questions that concern the operation of our food truck. During one of the interviews, I asked the applicant, "What other commitments do you have that might affect the operation?" I was surprised by many of the applicant's answers, as I expected a very formal and democratic answer. Some demanded to have their day off, and others replied with their travel plans and inability to work. I was furious from the inside, in the sense that you have not been accepted to lay your demands, and as if I am obligated to higher you so you can pay for you to rest. I wanted to give them a hard lesson, but I knew that the culture produced such behavior. Our culture has ingested the idea that we work to travel, and our monthly salary is granted, not compensation for the work contributed. And not that we are paid for our work, and that esteem comes from sweat and time we spend to earn the money we are paid. It is the fundamental meaning of living human beings; due to the limited resources, we work to survive.

After multiple wrongly picked candidates for the job, I have developed a model to pick the right employee. First, an interview that evaluates different aspects of the applicant, and on each question, a character rating is developed to measure the candidate's fit to our company. I learned the importance of measuring the person's character from Ray Dalio's book "Life Principals." Ray Dalio, founder of the multi-billion company Bridgewater, explains in his book the importance of the future employee's character. He explains that every company has set values for everyone to abide by and promote. And, we usually pick candidates wrongly because we only focus on skills and forget the values/character of the candidate and how it will fit in our company. For example, I was impressed by one candidate's portfolio; he was a dental student who knew how to talk and expressed his seriousness about working with us. I was going to immediately accept him until I asked him if he could work full-time for one week to see how serious he was. And he said that he had to be with his parents for at least three days a week. I would have picked him if I did not have a clear view of the values we were looking for. But, his commitment to the job was compromised because of his answer, which would have cost us a lot of time, effort, and money.

**"Pick the one with the character that
matches the company's values."**

5/19/2019

How do you motivate your Team?

I am sure many know Maslow's Law

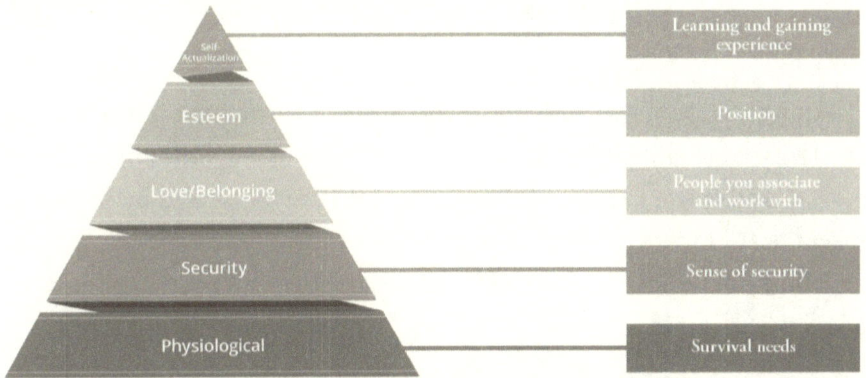

Maslow explains that the basic drive for people is the function of money (physiology), which allows us to buy the things that allow us to live. And, in every stage, people will try to reach the second stage to be motivated to work. For example, if physiology is granted, then security would be the second motivating factor for the continuation of work motivation which is acquiring security, and so on to Affiliation, and then to self-esteem (prestige) until you reach the tip of the pyramid, self-actualization.

Maslow explains that self-actualization is the ultimate motivator. We must evolve to keep producing as it gives us a sense of living. Self-actualization means that we allow our teams and employees the chance to learn, gain new skills, and lead projects. I can correlate self-actualization with children. In the most curious stage of life, we want to learn, touch everything we see, experience all kinds of walking methods, and speak with different voices. The same understanding can be related to retirees. Once they retire from their long working life, life surprises them with depression due to their inability to learn and experience new challenges.

I relate to self-actualization whenever I read a book and learn something new, as I feel the dopamine spreading into my body because I am evolving mentally. And, I understood the saying "money is not everything," because you see, Maslow did not mention wealth as a motivator; it is a by-product. I also wondered why many smart people were happy at low-paying jobs. But, I realized that money was never a motivational driver, and as long as they are evolving and feel fulfilled, they will be loyal to their job.

Another aspect was portrayed: the difference between jobs requiring creativity and skilled work (such as plant operator, salesman, driver, etc…). And it was explained that skilled jobs are motivated by monetary incentives. However, in the case of creative jobs, once they are granted an optimum salary, money will not be a future motivator supporting Maslow's pyramid.

**"How people are motivated changes with time.
Make sure you know how to motivate your team."**

Alasalah University recently interviewed me to tell the story of the food truck. Most of my answers were connected with the 5Ps.

1. Place

    Location, location, location. I explained that our process of choosing a location was not easy. The first step we took was acquiring data through a survey that we have shared with a selected customer base. In the survey, we asked some questions about location and where you live? And, where would you like it to be if we were to open a food truck? We then pulled a map of the city we targeted, and we started pinpointing the customers' answers.

    After we selected the areas that we want to analyze as a result of the survey, we took the car and drove around those areas to visualize the areas and confirm our analysis. We drove for hours and hours until we drove by a road called "Uthman Bin Affan."

I just felt it in my guts; the road lacked restaurants, and our targeted customers were either walking or driving on that road. I pictured our food truck parked on that road, and imagined customers waiting in line to order from our food truck.

Even though we picked the right area, we did not succeed in picking the right parking location at our initial opening. As we only sold three burgers on our first day. Thankfully we were a mobile food truck, and we managed to move the truck 0.5 km away from the first spot. Our sales jumped to 60 burgers per day. You won't realize the importance of the location until you try a bad one. People who say, "customers will come to you no matter where your location is," do not know what they are talking about.

2. People

You will have no customers if you do not target a specific segment of people. Knowing your customer means knowing your location, product pricing, and marketing approach. It is the social proof strategy. Think of amazon when it first started as an online bookstore with a specific target; book readers. Or Tesla, when it sold its car as a luxury car, which targeted wealthy people. And Google started as a search engine for people to access information easily. These companies had a specific customer to target, and were not generalists when they started their businesses.

3. Product

The nice thing about the 5ps is that they depend on each other. One cannot start a successful business without a business model linked to the 5Ps.

The product is your core business. If the product is not sellable, then the other 4ps are useless. It is like selling a Nokia in today's age of innovation. No one is going to budge for a Nokia. The people who bought Nokia 13 years ago are the same people who are buying iPhones today.

4. Promotion

In business, you never stop promoting. You are promoting your business when dealing with customers, through advertisement, and enhancing & improving your product. Promotion means you keep reminding your employees of your brand, product, and why they need to keep buying from you.

5. Price

Even when succeeding and generating revenue, price is a concern. You must study the pricing by knowing the market/competition and the targeted customer purchase power. People are sensitive to price, especially when it is increased after they start knowing your brand. When we started the food truck, we started at relatively high prices but were also competitive with the market prices.

At the beginning of the food truck, we reviewed our accounts and the impact of our product pricing. I remember increasing the price of two products due to a pricing disadvantage costing us a lot of profit loss. Although it was not the highest sold product, people questioned the price increase. And it was very hard to justify. However, since we first started increasing the product price, it did not impact us much. When you start your business, utilize the flexibility advantage of a new business to conduct price experiment.

Data…

Some say data is the new oil. Not in the sense that it was recently discovered, because it is not. Data and Data storage was available before the 1990s. However, we did not have the mechanisms to store a big chunk of data, as 1 MB of storage used to be very expensive.

Today, a small chip, the tip of the finger, can store more than 250 GB, a huge development in data storage. Previously, when we cross-referenced data, the data were insufficient to be analyzed. With the progress of data storage through either cloud or servers, we were more capable of storing big data and having them analyzed. Data allows enterprises, manufacturers, retailers, and so on to forecast sales, predict shot-downs, equipment repair, equipment performance, and many other analyses. Data has revolutionized the way to do business today; data drive everything.

In our business, we had to look for ways to utilize our data, specifically sale trends and customer experience, which could be developed through launching new products, marketing, packaging, lead-time of food readiness, and so on. Data would allow us to measure the development of our business. Many platforms made data analytics accessible (Koinz, Sprinklr, Zendesk, Yotop, Hootsuite, and plenty others). These platforms can capture reviews and customer feedback through social media and rating applications.

I remember one of the techniques we used when we launched a new product in the food truck. We added it to the menu for one day a week, playing two gambits, deprival syndrome, and projecting the sale trend for the product. This technique also allowed us to modify the product and play with its pricing without impacting the brand's image. Selling the product one day a week allowed us to hear customer feedback and develop the product to fit our customers' desires.

Data is important. We are using it today to forecast daily targets, which is very important in the Food and Beverage industry to avoid waste.

"Data is becoming the enabler of business."

Structure…

Without governance, rules & regulations, humans could not evolve to reach more than 7 billion in population. Imagine that your neighbor decides one day to expand his house beyond his land boundaries. He won't dare because there is a certificate of construction & land ownership that approves the constructed house's area, floor, and design. And this system will withstand in court as proof of the neighbor's misconduct. Easy!

However, back in the days of barbarian life, the case of neighbor would be solved by those with a stronger status and could reach to deadly fight — the same for any organization. An organization without guidelines, and rules & responsibilities, will promote a modern barbarian environment.

When we first started our food truck business, I remember we had no structure of responsibilities and rules for the employees to follow. For instance, when we hired our first employees, no orientation was given to set the ground for the employees' responsibilities and the company rules, which we did not know at the time. As a result, one employee acted as if he was working in his own house, where he could eat and drink at the company's expense. It was hard to discipline the employee because we thought it should be common sense. However, common sense does not act like a structure. Although the employee was later disciplined, ground rules were set at least verbally. It was an eye-opening experience that forced us to develop guidelines and structure the operation of the business. And, we made sure we do not make the same mistake again with our future employees. We started conducting orientations and explaining their responsibilities and the company's values that everyone must abide by.

The structure must be flexible in the sense that it evolves with time. Organizations are never static. They are continuously growing/declining and facing challenges that may affect operation. And so, the structure is not a government law; it is a tool that helps the manager and subordinates.

"Choose structure over barbarian."

7/1/2019

Are you feeling what you are feeling?

The "15 commitments to conscious leadership" book asks the leader to commit to feeling the feeling and exerting it out of your body. So the book indicates that leaders feel five emotions; Anger, Joy, Sadness, Sexual feelings, and Fear. Leaders often think that leaders must not exert their feeling and stop any feelings. However, this has made leaders unconscious leaders. Unconscious leaders do not build corporations and cultures.

A great example of stopping feelings from leaving your system is when you use the hose to rinse the lawn. You first stop the water from exiting by using your thumb, then you partially open and the water explodes by pressure.

Humans are emotional machines. We feel different kinds of emotions continuously. So what do you think would happen if you stopped your feelings? You cannot stop your feelings; they must leave your body and mind.

When we feel, we process our feelings in two different ways. We either:

A. Stop our body and mind from feeling the energy of our emotions, whether anger, fear, joy, sadness, or/or sexual. Stopping ourselves from feeling will drive us to two states. State 1: exploding our feelings uncontrollably. State 2: the feeling stays inside our system; I call it the black box. And the event reemerges now and then.

After remembering it, our mind reprocesses whatever we feel and gets trapped back in the black box. It is a cycle of destruction. If human beings do not forget, we will be devastated. Forgetting is a blessing.

B. We allow ourselves to feel the energy of our emotions and understand what and why we are feeling whatever we are feeling to be conscious leaders. Understanding the feeling, why we are feeling it, acknowledging it, and allowing it to leave our mind, and learning from it, will help us to move forward and build better relationships with our customers/employees/ family members.

Do not feel embarrassed by feeling your emotions, as they are the energy that allows us to inspire and be inspired, achieve our dreams, build relationships, and be happy. Feel your feelings, understand them and exert them. Do not trap them in your black box.

"Feel your Feelings"

7/21/19

Development...

Business development is vital for growth and sustainability. I would classify development into Quality, Expansion, New Ideas, and Team.

1. Quality development includes increasing the efficiency of the business and implementing new programs/systems. Every process has gaps that require refinement to improve the quality. For example, in our food truck business, food quality is critical for the business to prosper. And to have sustainable quality standards, we developed a procedure that will allow us to govern processes within the business by following the below guidelines:

- Employee responsibility shall be clearly defined and communicated visually and verbally. The best way to outline responsibilities is to be in the field of operation and visualize the ideal procedure.

- The procedure must be concise and follows a step-by-step sequence.

- The procedures and systems are not written stone. Management must be flexible with new modifications. However, it must be captured and communicated with the team.

Imbedding new technologies and quality checks is a fabulous resource for quality development.

2. Expansion. Every successful business thinking of growth has expanded its business plan. It is fairly straightforward as it can be by opening new branches and/or reaching a bigger audience. Below are considerations when setting a strategy for expansion:

    - Location

    - Resources

    - Workforce

    - Marjeting strategy

3. New Ideas. Implementing new ideas mostly deals with new ways to increase profit streams, mainly under two umbrellas; new products and/or innovative marketing.

4. Team development is the most important of all development elements as they are the business drivers for better outcomes.

- Team synergy and having the right employees believe in the company's values.

- Availing the right resources.

- Providing enough guidance.

- Communicating clearly and thoroughly.

- Implementing retreat events.

- Developing their knowledge and competencies.

Continuous development is the main factor in business survival. If ignored or undervalued, the business is planning for its end.

"Developing is survival."

CHAPTER 6

OPPORTUNITIES

8/8/2019

When I look ten months back and think of the businesses I have evaluated to pursue, I feel like my fear is playing mind games. I felt like I was walking away from money-making ideas because I convinced myself that the cons outweighed the pros. Is what I am feeling true? Or am I overthinking its effects? A question that I could not answer. I have done multiple decision-making tools such as Kepner Tregoe, SWOT Analysis, Pros & Cons breakdown, and discussions with Subject Matter Expertise. These have helped to understand the business ventures and identify some challenges. However, when people are inquired about their view of the business, the mind is wired to focus on pain. The mind usually records what is painful and what is joyful. There is nothing wrong with how the mind is wired, as recording pain helps us grow and avoid such circumstances in the future. But, if you are trying to understand the pain of someone else's experience, it becomes hard to evaluate their view and you start to build a story of your own from their perspective.

What if they are right? Is this business not profitable? What if they are complainers or loss-averse is clouding their jusdgments? And the story becomes either pragmatic or misleading. I have always said you have to ask the right people. For instance, if you want to check if you have cancer, you can't go to an engineer to perform the required tests to check your health. If you are considering starting a service business, you must ask people in the same industry you are servicing.

Make sure you have a process to understand your emotions, do not just believe every word you here. I remember my father, a successful man who built a legacy under his name. Before I started the food business, my father was not buying into food services. He advised me to get into manufacturing and something that people will always buy. However, a year into the business, he changed his mind and started advising me to get into services rather than manufacturing. Although he is in the manufacturing business, has been a CEO of different companies, and has held different positions within some of the biggest companies in Saudi Arabia, his opinion of the right business was based on his emotions and experiences and not on a thorough evaluation.

We, humans, are driven by the energy of emotions. I was reading a book, 15 commitment to leadership, which stated that we have five types of emotions; Joy, Sadness, Fear, Sexual feelings, and Anger. And, we need to recognize these feelings that others also feel. And, when they speak, they express feelings that may or may not distort the story.

"Consolidate, process your emotions, and think clearly to have a pragmatic story."

9/25/19

It was not easy to negotiate …

In the past two months, I have worked on an opportunity in medical and wellness services. And the business was intriguing as it is in a market valued at more than $0.5 trillion worldwide. As well as the diversity of the products provided by the company we are trying to partner with from weight loss, medical products and equipment, and workplace wellness products.

When we had consolidated all of the information provided by the company, we needed to evaluate the business, and the time had come to negotiate terms. Both parties were focused on developing a partnership agreement, and I believe we have not faced any issues regarding the agreement terms. However, the other party was not approving our proposed partnership fee since it is formulated as a master license agreement. We were trying to lower the licensing fee to ensure we had the cash to cover the expenses for the year ahead. In contrast, the other party is receiving devaluation alarms which complicated negotiations.

We took the following negotiation gambits:

1. We had not agreed or disagreed with the fee even when it was reduced.
2. Used higher authority gambit (I have to consult my partner, check with the government regulations, and we will get back to you…)
3. Propose more than one proposal for the other party's consideration, preferably two.
4. Ask for more than what you want. Make sure the offers are more than what you desire. So when you negotiate, you can compromise on the decision you have been targeting.
5. Take time, set your deadline, and ensure you are prepared to counter.
6. Make sure you are prepared to have a counter offer strategy if you negotiate through a conference call. The strategy is points 1 to 4.
7. Respect all offers and do not be offended.
8. Understand your position and the counter party's position.

"Negotiate your terms and fight the fear of loss inside you."

9/1/2019

I have been offered a managerial path…

I did not expect a call from my manager, a longtime friend of my father's, and he asked to meet me. I came to his office that day, and he expressed his interest in putting a plan for my career to be on track for a manager position in 10 years. I was also impressed when I felt depressed because I couldn't accept the offer. I have been planning to build a business outside the company for a long time, solely driven by a passion for entrepreneurship. However, being on track for a manager is an offer many may dream of.

I would not have felt depressed if the offer was not proposed. The idea is, what if I turned down the offer and if my dream to build a business outweighs the losses. No decision is 100% gain. We have to lose to gain. We have to taste something bitter to differentiate what sweet is.

Gain:

1. Leaving the corporate world will allow me to be my boss.
2. Hiring the people that I want to work with.
3. Building a strategy that will make me proud.
4. Creating the environment that would allow me to be fulfilled.
5. Developing myself in the field of my interest and choosing, and not because of the person I report to.
6. 10x experience by being an entrepreneur.

Losses:

1. Salary and benefits.
2. Security.
3. My father's network.

Security plays with the human mind, pushing it away from getting into risky ventures. Many what ifs and scenarios are formulated that occupy my mind, thinking this will be the end. However, the mind does not vision a prosperous venture and benefits that will be present when going into business and quitting a good-paying job. And that is how my mind is pushing me to quit on my dream and stick to my job. However, the gains will give me the freedom I desire to enter new ventures.

Will I fail or succeed? That is the question I ask myself every moment to ensure I make the right decision. But who can predict the future? If we were able to outline the future, life would be boring. And so, I asked myself a different question; will I regret not trying to pursue something that I believe will/may allow me to have the life I desire? Regret will be the case. Failing on something I wanted to try is better than failing on something I never tried.

Will I regret trying what I think will bring freedom and satisfaction? Maybe we will see in three years. Failure is bitter, but it is not the end of the world.

"Try and acknowledge your loss aversion, mind."

11/20/2019

I travelled to the states with more than a 15-hour flight to assess a boutique fitness specialising in spinning sports classes. My sister, who pursues sport as a passion, is interested in franchising a business stationed in the united states. Although the idea of spinning classes is not new, the boutique business model is fairly new in Saudi Arabia. It is built on that community, entertainment, and quick workout concept.

I directed the team to assess the company and see if it is an opportunity in Saudi Arabia. Our visit focused on three pillars: management, customer experience, and competitive advantage.

Management: It is always hard to judge a team in three days and not be emotional. However, the team had synergy and passion from the two days we had spent on socializing and business meetings. Each team member loved what they did and explained their discipline well. In any team, you will know if they have synergy by being aligned with the goal of the business. The presence and contribution of the founders are also very important as they construct the company's vision. Another factor that we focused on to assess the business is measuring the company's performance. In other words, how do you know that the company is being managed in the right direction?! And, I believe the business we were assessing failed to present programs that would allow us to evaluate the business's performance (KPIs), which should not be difficult to build and implement.

Customer Experience: How does the customer feel when they ride in that studio?

I would say I felt the energy when I rode that bike. The instructor, the soul of the business, did a good job of making the workout smooth and fun.

Are they feeling entertained?

The main competitive advantage of the spinning studio concept is working out entertainingly. I compared the adrenaline stimulation that should have happened when riding to concerts. In a concert, the beat starts by being slow to prepare the audience, and once the high beat hits, everyone jumps and pumps the blood and injects that happy feeling. Well, that was not something I saw or felt in that room.

Is it serving its purpose, which is making people more fit?

I think that was achieved as the whole participant in the workout was sweating.

I would say when you get into a partnership; an important quality is understanding and acceptance. Founders sometimes feel that they have built a golden opportunity and would feel that nothing is going wrong in their operation. However, the company we visited accepted and understood the validity of our comments, and I am sure they will figure out a way to be better managers.

Information will never be enough to know if a business is successful. However, knowing 70% of a business is enough to make a decision. One thing that is left that we will be assessing is the financial aspect of the company and its franchisees. (P&Ls, cash-flow)

One thing I find improving in myself is the mind over emotion factor. It is very important to understand your emotions, assess the business from different views, and do not cloud your judgments by what you hear (trust but verify).

"It is very important to understand your emotions and assess a business with different views and not cloud your judgments by what you hear" (search for: Reasoning misjudgment)

CHAPTER 7

2020

2/11/2020

Discipline….

Discipline is a habit; it is not necessarily a mindset. Sometimes we get surprised at how specific people have accomplished challenging tasks. Not because they are not capable, but because they are either incompetent or uneducated. However, we see the common thing in successful people; they are disciplined to deliver and reach their targets. You could say persistence or determination. However, discipline is something that is instilled in our day-to-day routine.

As an entrepreneur who seeks to achieve great things, I have been fighting with my own mind to create a successful routine that keeps me inspired and disciplined. It is hard! At one point, you think you are doing the right thing by reading a book to increase your business knowledge. On the other hand, you think that you are doing it at the expense of the business. I know what you will be thinking, balance. However, balance cannot be quantified. And, it will always feel like your balance is tilted towards one end more than the other.

Discipline is not on actions only, but the thoughts that get into your mind and your way of processing the information to be rational, which then translates into actions, which is not easy to get accustomed to.

3/1/2020

We had to change our location!

The location where we have been operating our food truck for three years is no longer feasible. The road is under maintenance. The roads are peeled off, and there is no way the food truck can continue in its current location for the foreseeable future because the customers won't be able to park their cars to order.

I was working the night shift 45 minutes away from the city. I had no time to deal with the business situation. However, we had to act fast. And so, we changed the location to somewhere close to the original location, less attractive and distanced us from our original customers. We had to change our strategy and find another location that would be as good. But it is not that simple; in the original location, we built a following and loyal customer base who strive to eat from us. How are we going to rebuild that somewhere else? It was devastating. It felt like we lost the business. I felt like a little boy who changed school. By the way, I changed schools every three years, and it was hard to make new friends.

However, location is the biggest factor in business, especially in the food industry, which could create or break the business. We were fighting for survival and weren't going to give up easily, which is the beauty of a food truck; we can change our location to find a better one. But, when you have built an operation around the business, operation expenses increase the risk of losing it all.

By God's grace, we found a location that will allow us to survive the wind. We have to work on it, but it is better than nothing.

"Make sure you build a great ship to withstand hurdles and challenges. What do you need to survive the wind? Because you will be facing many."

5/9/20

This year is the hardest for governments, enterprises, employees, and citizens globally. COVID-19, the virus that we have very little information about, has changed how we live. It started at the beginning of the year but reached an alarming point in mid-March. Everyone was panicking; countries started closing industries, sending people home, and implementing lockdown precautions. Mid-March, our food truck business was affected, but we survived with enough revenue to pay our dues. However, at the end of March, the government started a 24hrs lockdown, which technically put us out of business. Fortunately, we pushed at full speed, advertising our "grill your burger" at home, which thankfully reduced the expense burden and helped us to survive April. These times are very devastating. I would say that I have hopes for what follows after the COVID-19 virus fears lay down and lockdown restrictions are lifted. But, when will the consumer purchasing behavior recovers? And, when will the unemployed get their jobs back? These questions may not have an answer because time only will prevail.

The Stock market slumped 25-30%. Some predict V-shaped recovery; others believe U-shaped and L-shaped. Everyone expects different crisis and have different reactions. In our case, do we start building our restaurant? Do we release our employees without pay? There are no indications or signs of the best move. At one point, you feel like taking the risk is the best choice; at another, different feelings prevail, tilted to being more risk-averse and taking extra measures for the business to live longer. I do not know what the future holds from an economic point of view, especially in the food industry. Will food businesses transform their operation more towards automation? Is it going to be 100% delivery? If that is the case, we should focus on logistics and customer reach, rather than building restaurants.

I hope for a better future, but it seems to be hard. Oil was sold for less than 20$, so Saudi has started tightening its spending, making the market outlook even worse.

I was looking into new opportunities, but with everything that is going on, I wonder about the right business to start. Is there a depression down the road? Many economists predict that things will not get back quickly, high unemployment, and people's behavior will change to a point where they spend less and save more.

6/1/2020

Two months since the lockdown started due to the Covid-19 pandemic, many jobs have been lost, and the market is the most volatile in history. This time makes you recalculate your plans and how you see the business environment. Did people's behavior change? Are we going to survive in the food truck business? Will the business prosper? Do we exit the market and collect our gains? Or keep fighting? A lot of confusion within the market. No one alive today has experienced such a market situation since the Spanish flow. And, no one has the simplest idea of what is to come. It is estimated that 72% of food services have been wiped out during this pandemic!

As a business owner, I think of the past struggles we have overcome from government regulations, imposing new taxes, expense increases, and partnership meltdown, and using it to get some strength in such times. In other words, I am trying to shift our mindset from Freeze/Flee to fighting mode. I believe it is called the survival of the fittest. If we survive an event that happens every century, then nothing will stop us.

We had seven employees, which is a relatively very low number of employees, and because of the crisis we are going through, three employees were released from their duties, unfortunately. The other four employees' salaries were cut in half when many other businesses relieved employees with no pay. Fortunately, we had reserved some capital for the new store project that we put on hold to withstand the market blow, which has also allowed us to be leaner and optimize our operations & expenses.

Another shocking news aired recently is the sales tax increase from 5% to 15%. Though many countries, during market stresses, incentivize consumer spending by lowering interest rates and taxes, it was not the case here in Saudi.

What happens when taxes increase, many jobs are lost, expenses increase, and revenue plummets? People panic at this point and sell out. However, if we think about the future, the big pie gets smaller, and many players in the market will have to shutdown as they cannot withstand the overhead. This technically allows the small business to fill the gap if they have a good strategy and enough capital to cover their small overhead compared to big companies. Are we scared? No doubt. Are we risking our time and investment? You bet.

"Life is a cycle. The market is also the best form of a cycle; it has its ups and downs. What will you do about it? And, how will you be prepared when times are tough, and investors are running for their lives?"

7/4/2020

When expenses increase, should you increase your prices?

This is a question many businesses struggle to answer. The truth is there is no correct answer. However, there is a strategy that leads to an answer.

Will the increase in expenses exceed my breakeven point?

In the long term, are you going to recover from added costs?

Who is your customer? Middle class, average income, rich…

We did see that our expenses in the long term will not be in our favor if we do not increase our prices. We have also learned from the previous 5% tax increase that a wave of price increases will hit the market. And, we saw how people reacted then to price increases. The first reaction would be resentment, acceptance will follow, and some will change their behavior. However, if company A increases its prices, people will blame the tax rather than the company's greed. Customers who want the product and can pay for it will still buy it and adjust their budget to bear the increased expenses. That is a good scenario, but in reality, many companies fail and shutdown because their customers cannot bear the cost and will give up their desire or shift their behavior to a lower class.

Say, for example, a middle-class customer who eats in fancy restaurants every two days. Once prices increase, the customer will either reduce the number of times he eats in fancy restaurants to once a week or shift to casual dining. And so forth for other classes.

Though we are still testing our market with our new prices due to the 15% sales taxes, we have bared the cost of 5% and left 10% for customers to pay. And, we have advertised for our initiative to ensure customers are aware of the discount we are providing. The feedback is relatively positive.

CHAPTER 8

BEYOND 2020 CRISIS

11/27/2020

New Store, New struggles

Turnover of employees is a challenging part of the food business in particular.

It has been more than a year since we started planning for the shift from a food truck to a store. We have contracted with a very slow, unprofessional agency to work on developing our new brand, store design, and menu. We have made two mistakes here. The first is paying upfront for all the services instead of breaking the payments on deliverable bases, which would have allowed us to assess the agency and be firmer with any lags or unsatisfying results. However, in our case, because we had paid them in advance, we were under their mercy, and we played under their rules which frustrated us a lot along the way. The second mistake was giving the agency all the development scope, which is incorrect. A brand designer differs from a store designer, and a menu developer is unrelated to visual designs. This has resulted in average results and a lot of iterations along the way. We fell for convenience and trusted the agency's perceived competency. Thankfully, we have completed the scope with a strong force to build something we admire.

Building a store is not an easy task, and it is different from a food truck, which indicates that we need to acquire new skills and a new approach to food presentation and modernize the brand. We have learned from the agency's mistakes, and made sure not to repeat it when contracting with a construction agency. Believing that you will not make a mistake is nonsense in business. And, we need to pay attention to our psychological state of mind when making decisions to be aware and learn from our mistakes.

In the food sector, it is known that there is a high turnover of employees. I am still trying to figure out the reason. Losing a productive employee is devastating for the business owner, especially when dealing with food, because your customer will immediately feel the difference. I like Starbucks, and I usually give examples of how they operate. If you go to Starbucks, you will find that quality is maintained even if an employee is changed due to a rigid system emplaced in the company brand essence. Another thing that Starbucks does is rotate their employees, so the customer doesn't get attached to the employee, but the brand makes it less problematic when the employee decides to move out.

Though one of our values is quality, it is hard to build value within the business if employee turnover is high. With every new employee, you have to start from the beginning, which is what we are currently struggling with. We have new employees, and we start teaching them from scratch what is expected and how the brand essence should look to set a stage for what is expected from them.

11/29/2020

27

I just turned 27. Where was I 4 years ago, and where am I today. Though I always think of the future and where I want to be, today, it is different. I am thinking of what I have accomplished and if I am getting closer to a goal. We believe that goals come in handy to high achievers, but it is not, and that's why you see many highly successful people who say they were lucky. But, the drive, strive, and hard work to create something is the key to success. We all want to do something in our lives, but are we working on achieving them?

Reaching 27 made me feel that I am getting closer to 30, but at the same time, feeling numb to the number 27. Though the feeling of getting older shifted my thinking to prosperity rather than risk, I still feel that time is ahead and life is short. I know that if I do not do what I think is best for myself, I will regret it. But, what is best for me? It is a question that pulls me from one string to the other. At some point, I feel it is indecisiveness; at another, I feel it is logical.

I have been waiting for the moment satisfaction, but I think the moment is something that we create with our minds. The moment is a journey. I say that because it is something I had encountered when I set a goal to quit my job and haven't done so when I reached the goal.

Reaching 27 has made me think of what is important in life? Family, friends, good lifestyle, and a meaningful life. It does not matter how much we have if we have the right people around us and are satisfied. But is it so? I think that is what we hear in every life podcast. Money doesn't matter, but it does. And what we need to understand is that we don't need to be rich; we need to be financially free. That is the goal that we shall strive for. And, we will not form that mindset as long as we compare ourselves with others. Wealth can be achieved simply by spending less than what you earn, saving, and investing to achieve financial freedom.

What is the difference between 27 and 37 or 47? I thought it was just a number. What will I think/feel when I am 37?

"Life is short; live it by the terms that fit your dream and would allow you to be thankful ten years from now" – I wish there was a formula, but uncertainty has good taste and allows us not to stop dreaming.

11/30/2020

Nurturing a leader

It is very challenging to pick a leader, and it is even more challenging to nurture one. I always try to figure out the leader's incentive buttons. Which is it from Moslow's law?

I have assigned a leader, who started as a normal employee, then promoted to supervisor, and now he is a general manager. We are a small company, so titles do not matter, but the responsibilities matter. We are at a stage where we must move quickly and effectively. And so, I do not know how I can motivate Saud to unleash his potential, develop more skills, and take the business to new highs. Should I become forceful and pushy? Or should I become lenient and be more meritocratic?

I am choosing to be lenient at the moment, and when I see areas of improvement, I discuss them. The fear of scaring him out pushes me back from overachieving the outcomes. At the same time, feelings are very powerful, and knowing so makes me careful of what to say, so we do not reach an undesirable situayion, especially if the person in front of me is not emotionally intelligent.

The expectation of a leader is high, and I have seen some traits that show a lack of leadership which brings me to the question of how to guide and reform Saud.

I have had different leaders throughout the business. Many of them left. And some are still in contact with me and help me out. I think I left a mark in their lifes as I guided them to become better leaders. I used not to give chances for improper actions and immediately highlight them. I believe that it has set a stage for what is expected, ensured we are building a professional business and that everyone working for it is expected to meet those standards. Employers think that employees are born professional, and so they will act like one without training them to do so. However, that is not right. Employees who do not have leadership instilled within them expect their employer to tell them how they should be better leaders. I have trained many employees, some staying for one day and others staying for two years or more. I learned that you could nurture a leader but you must instill leadership skills within them. I have tried many gadgets to empower and instill leadership, so many did not know it, but they couldn't be one. They had the desire, but they did not behave like one.

I concluded that the an employer could only know a potential leader, if he instills the company's values and encourage the leaders to continue behaving like one.

**"Leadership can be nurtured if the desire
and discipline traits are in the person's blood."**

12/1/2020

Today was the first day to operate our second truck since March 2020. We stopped the second truck due to the pandemic, but even when things opened up in July, it was hard to operate the truck without knowing the business's cash flow since many aspects changed. And we want to operate while we are financially strong.

I was driving the truck, as I had not driven it for so long, and memories flashed back to the beginnings. Things were tough by then and consumed much of my energy. In reality, I was an operator, not a business owner, not from an ego standpoint, but a business point of view. If you are a business owner and the business is doing well, you must start delegating and start focusing on developing and building a company.

When we reached the location, we started cleaning the truck and turning on the grill to serve. People's reception has struck me. I was surprised and delighted to see people stopping by the truck and asking where we had been and that they had missed eating our food. I felt like we lived in this neighborhood; my heart was pumping so fast, trying to understand what we had built here. Customers' reception felt like they are welcoming a family member.

I realized that we had struck a nerve in this neighborhood. We have left a mark in their memories, and they wanted to relive the old memories they had experienced from previous craves, dinners and hangouts. It was remarkable. The ultimate achievement in the consumer product business made them feel good when eating our product and leaving a memorable experience. There was one woman that touched my heart as she stopped by, she did not order food but wanted to stop by to welcome us, and said, "We missed you." I was stunned. I think I would say that to a friend, a family member, whom I haven't seen for a long time. But hearing it from our customers has amplified our vision of what we can build, and we formed a cult-like following of customers.

"Customer Experience" was and still is a tremendous value for the business we are trying to build. And achieving it will require building a culture that is so strong and workers embracing it first, then transforming it into the form of food.

**"You will not see the value of what you build
until you change your angle."**

12/2/2020

Cash flow & Financial Stability

We are currently developing the store and struggling with cash flow and managing expenses. It is tough. We estimated to have a 60K budget deficit without the turnover cost & recruitment, printable, maintenance, and other costs. Financial management is a fundamental key to business success, mainly managing cash flow.

We have committed ourselves to many contracts. Not because we aim to, but because we have to. Opening a restaurant and developing a new brand requires high investments. I am highlighting this because I fear we might not leave room for abrupt expenses. I contradict a financial thought mentioned in this book, but sometimes we must take risks. If we do not do so in a fast-moving world, we will miss out on opportunities.

Though we have created systems to track our cashflows and ensure financial stability, the question is what we can do to pump up revenue to reduce the expense burden. As I mentioned, we have reoperated the second truck and focused more on advertising our BBQ box to supplement our revenue streams further.

Long term view

I noticed yesterday that we lack a future view. We are more reactive than proactive. I think that human capital is the primary pillar of stability. If the right people are employed, and minimum employee retention is achieved, fewer business interruptions and more proactive actions are taken. This will increase our long-term view, and we shall exhaust our efforts to develop a system that incentivizes employees to stay longer in the company.

12/5/2020

Do you want to give up?!

It is the feeling of defeat, exhaustion, or being lost. I have felt that feeling multiple times and still don't know when that feeling will go away.

Today I am feeling that feeling because I fear losing. What if all the money we worked very hard to earn goes into the smoke because we are expanding? We are spending all of the savings left and right. We thought at first that building a restaurant would cost not more than 300K. We did not consider labor recruitment, rent, appliances, AC, etc. We are very close to 500K as of the moment, and more expenses are expected. I would not say it was poorly planned because it is a new business venture, and we have very limited experience in the restaurant business. Our expertise is more in food trucks; though the two businesses have similarities, they have many differences.

The feeling can only be seen as a bad stage in business. It is something that constrains the business and may be at a downfall. Getting yourself out of that misery is very important, but what is more important is recognizing that feeling and understanding it. I will list some tips that I use when I feel like giving up:

1. Get out of your comfort zone. Maybe do something different, or go to a different coffee shop. Or, eat at a very expensive restaurant. Walk at the beach. It will release the limiting thoughts inside your mind.
2. Go out and see friends & Family. Do not think of work or what needs to be done tomorrow.
3. Volunteer.

The feeling dims, I believe, when I hear encouraging customer feedback on our business. It also dims when I see others who do not have meaning in life. This pumps my energy and pushes me to want more than I have or reach higher grounds.

The state of mind is very vital for entrepreneurial survival. In reality, our minds have settings that send alarms once breached. These alarms can be detrimental or life-changing. It depends on what to do and how to react to them. The feeling of giving up is one of these settings, and allowing it to overwhelm our mind is like sending a fare well to the business.

12/7/2020

Exhaustion and thermostat

How does an Air Condition work? You have a thermostat that measures the temperature in the room and automatically turns off or on the compressor, meaning blow cold air or stop blowing. In retrospect, humans have many thermostats; thermostat for anger, thermostat for tiresome, thermostat for endurance, and so on.

Our minds set limits to ensure we do not overwork our bodies and damage them. In the past, cave dwellers worked hard to survive and acquire daily food. Imagine if they do not have a limit set to stop looking for food when their body is tired and lost a lot of water in the process, they would collapse, faint, and may die. It is like saying a car can drive without fuel. And So, setting limits is a blessing. However, that is why people say the worst enemy of yourself is you. I face that limiting feeling when trying to do physical activities or learning. I reach a stage where my mind says, "you had enough," when I know I can do much more. As a result, we set limits that stop us from overreaching high ground in our life, whether socially or financially.

In our world, life is much easier than it used to be in the cave dwellers' world. People used to live without eating for many days. In today's world, the fuel is productivity, contribution, and having the right people around you. Our minds are very old and store many settings that go back to when life started on earth. It would be nice if we had a software update such as apple store or google play, that would be nice, and our lives would transform. But, the real world would require more than that.

To change our settings, the best way to set our limits broader and higher is to train our minds and increase the settings a bit by bit. Slight improvement of our limiting thermostats would allow us to understand our potential and learn how our body and mind work intertwined. It is like our body is the moving parts, and our mind is the engine. You will achieve better outcomes if you fuel that engine with great thoughts and ways to expand.

It sounds simple, but I always struggle to teach my mind to have more stamina because, in the end, we are humans. We are not robots.

"Our minds are so old that has settings of old humans. We need to update them to 21st-century software."

Coosma & e-commerce

12/10/2020

We started an e-commerce website that failed!

The idea of the website was to offer cosmetic products and sell them for a price that is less than pharmacies. The other advantage that we aimed to offer was to ship fast. When we started the business, I knew that price usually is not a value proposition, especially if the product is not replacing an existing product. The products we were selling are available everywhere. And so, the only thing we provided the customer was the price advantage.

We started planning in May 2020, and the website was up and running in August 2020. Everything was quick. We found suppliers, and our warehouse was set up quickly. We hired relatively competent employees. However, the number of products was so high that we could not identify which would attract customers to buy from the website. Our website alone had 2000+ products. I believe that one of the main advantages we had is not having inventory. We offered many products, and we only purchased the product from the market when customers ordered them; this was our strategy. We wanted to understand consumer behavior and the best-selling products to know what we need to stock.

When the website was up and running, it was frustrating to see no sales. Opening a website is similar to setting up a store in the sky; no one will see it unless you strongly advertise for it. And, so we started Facebook ads. But, it did not work as we hoped it would. Customers from Facebook were only browsing the website, but they didn't buy anything. The feeling of not having sales was devastating. We did not know what was wrong. We then decided to do influencer marketing, receiving a huge number of orders, but we did not know that it would take tremendous effort to buy and ship the products. Imagine 20 orders, and each order will have 4 to 10 items, and for you to source them in the market, you have to stop by the stores that may or may not have them. We sometimes buy products similar to the customer's order because the market does not have the exact item. It was another devastating outcome that hit our business model pretty hard.

The other thing that made our business hopeless was the high number of returned orders and unhappy feedback we received from customers. Because we either delivered the wrong products, or the products were fake, which is a whole other story. We then decided to close down the business. In 2 months, we built the business from scratch, and two months later, we shut it down. We learned a lot from the failure.

We were excited initially, but our business model had many flaws. And, we had a lot of competition that is a replica of our business model, leaving us with no advantage. I will share some of the lessons learned from this experience.

12/11/2020

Lessons learned from opening an e-commerce website!

1. Don't make price alone your main value proposition, unless it is an invention, business model that can't be replicated easily, or a new product.

    Our prices were 20% less than many of the competitors in the market. We thought that reducing the price by this much would surely incentivize the customer to buy from us. Though we knew that other players had the same business model we had thought of, we did not know that we had to differentiate ourselves from the market. We also forgot that we had to gain consumer confidence to build an e-commerce website, which is very hard when operating on the internet. It is much easier to interact in person and convince the customer to buy. But, how can you achieve so on the internet? We had chatting services, and we did provide our social media accounts. We also provided our commerce registration to show that we are a legit business. But customers wanted to know that our products are originals and be confident they will be delivered.

    At first, we believed that our suppliers would sell original products. However, we were doomed once we found that many products were not originals. One of the main factors to incentive customers to buy from us is no longer valid.

2. Make sure your business model works! And, I mean work!

    As I have said, our business model revolved around the idea of not buying any stock. We will buy what the customer orders. However, when the customer ordered, we didn't know if we would find it in the market, and that is where we found flaws in our business model. We assumed that the products would be available in the wholesale market. We sometimes searched for the products for days but couldn't find them. It was frustrating because the idea of not having inventory is a fundamental pillar of our business model. Our customers were not happy. We were confused, and we did not know what would work. Now I know that this is the beauty of a startup; you can iterate easily, but pivoting at that point was difficult mentally and physically.

3. Do not open an everything store unless you are an everything store!

Before we opened the online store, we thought, if we provided everything considered as necessary cosmetics such as shampoos, creams, pampers, gels, you name it, we would reach everyone. We did have a segment of people we wanted to target, but our strategy to have an everything store confused our customers. We did not know what people bought. And, we thought if we had an everything store, we would attract everyone, which is a poor strategy. We knew that targeting everyone is a plan that is doomed to fail. Knowing but not acting on our beliefs confused us more. I will be honest that this is the main thing that made me think we needed to close down the business because I did not know what to focus on. We made very low sales (3-5 orders per week!). I think even our customers did not feel they should buy from us and compared us to other stores that were more efficient and trustworthy.

4. Marketing for an e-commerce business!

The hardest thing to do in an online business is marketing. However, once you get the gits of it, it becomes handy.

We suffered a lot. We had a high stream of visitors to our store through Facebook ads. Customers were adding items to their carts daily without checking out. We even tried to call them to see why they had not made a purchase, and we got responses that did not make sense "well, I might get back to buy," "oh yeah, I know your store, Nothing is wrong, but I am still thinking about buying." We thought that people enjoyed the process but did not feel like checking out, which meant that their intentions were browsing out of boredom.

In other words, we were attracting the wrong crowd.

We then tried different audiences, and we developed different attractive content. We had sales but they very minimum. We did not know what would work, we were experimenting with no luck. This goes back to the everything store. If we had products that differentiated us from another website, we would have focused our efforts on marketing those products. But, in our case, what do we choose? We had +2000 products.

5. Shipping!

Shipping was another mess on its own. We thought sorting was simple, but when you get multiple orders, it becomes very challenging. Dealing with shipping agencies was another mess; we had to meet their schedule and pick-up time. One thing that struck me as a difficulty is when an order is returned to us because the customer did not pick up their order, we then had to try another time or another day.

Another part of logistics that we faced many issues with was the product's condition once the customer received the package. We did not know how to control it. I believe we would have solved the issue along the way had we continued operating the business.

12/13/2020

Marketing Challenges for the food trck business

Oh boy! I thought we knew how to market, but things are way much harder than I thought. As I have introduced, we have changed our food truck location from where we have been for almost three years. Now we are in a new location with many new customers trying our food and still do not know what we offer. However, with competition around us, marketing is the game. We will only prove strong at our current location if we are strong in marketing.

I thought marketing was something we have been good at and knew very well, but it is way more challenging than I thought. We have been expanding our reach through social media, creating campaigns, and focusing on the customer experience, like building a compelling seating area. Our sales had improved by single digits, but our expectations are way higher. We are currently working on creating digital menus using monitors to reduce the decision time and provide live pictures of our menu to attract more customers.

Marketing is the game for any business, and it changes in time. I remember changing our approach in social media ads from animated graphics to lifestyle pictures, and today we have transformed our brand to be more modern which gives us more of an upscale look. As part of our branding strategy, we also decided to have our logo and brand essence on our packaging supplies to capture the customer's experience when ordering, carrying the food, and eating. That will permanently engrave our brand essence in our customers' minds. I remembered a story that I heard from one of our new customers. He was an old man and used to see his kids come to the house several times with small boxes. The boxes caught the old man's eyes, and he wondered what these were for. So when the old man accidentally stopped by our food truck, he saw these boxes and busted out laughing; and he told me the story about the boxes and was highly intrigued to try our food. That is the power of branding.

Renewing and modernizing is a great tool to market your brand. However, there is a risk in doing so. Take Coca-Cola, for example; they have not changed their bottle design for decades. An experiment was done to test the customer experience. A group of people were brought into a lab setting and installed a machine in their heads that captured brain activity. Then, they let them drink the Coca-Cola from a glass, but nothing was observed from the brain waves. Another group was asked to drink the Coca-cola drink from the can itself. And here, the group had brain waves that showed the participant had a good experience. This intern means that the can colors and brand triggered customers' happiness from drinking the cola. And so, cola drinkers linked the good feeling that they experience from drinking a cola with the cans because that is the best way the mind can trigger a happy experience.

"To create an experience, mix brand and taste to engrave pictures and snaps in your customer's mind."

12/15/2020

25% reduction on yesterday's sales in the food truck!

Whenever I see the numbers of sales dropping, my heart drops, and I start fearing the current situation and exploring options to boost sales. It is normal in the food business to see such drops on a specific day or season. The feelings are so real and frightening. My heart is pumping fast, trying to understand the situation and hoping for a better day tomorrow.

We did suffer a lot in the past months, from changing location, the virus outbreak, employee lay-offs, and many other factors. I feel like we are in a hole and we are trying to get out of it, but instead, we are digging a deeper hole by opening a restaurant, risking our financial stability. We, as of the moment, have a budget deficit of 80,000 Riyals. I know it is very small compared to the other big companies with millions and billions in deficit. But it is no difference if you do a ratio analysis.

There is something that we are not doing right, obviously, marketing. We came up with different ideas, but none have made a drastic change. We are not meeting our targets from our marketing efforts. What is wrong? I am unaware and know we have a better product than our competitor. I also know that we have a better brand. Or else I am being blindsided by who we think we are. Is there a marketing secret that we are not doing?

It feels like someone is kicking me from the back. I am not able to understand why things are not working as we hoped. We will see; I hope things will turn around. I also hope that we will not face financial trouble.

12/17/2020

Thoughts are rushing like a roller coaster!

I do not know why, but my mind blows with creative ideas and solves problems when I drive. On many occasions, when I am facing hard challenges, I feel that my mind is stuck somewhere, but when I drive, my mind gets very active somehow, and thoughts come rushing to my mind. My heart pumps in excitement. I am ready to fly and break all the walls in my way. I wish this excitement could be accessed when I am executing projects or when fear and worry overwhelms me.

One day, I was stuck on our food truck's brand design and outlook, and I couldn't think or get into the creative side of my mind. Then, I was going for a drive to my hometown on a weekend, and I had this ecstasy moment where my mind just kept throwing ideas and painting pictures of what the truck could look like. My mind was flying with thoughts, I remember even noting down the ideas on whatever paper I could find in the car to make sure I did not forget, and I sketched the food truck picture and brand essence. I loved driving to my hometown that day because it allowed my mind to get into a stage of creativity. This moment has happened a lot after, on different problems.

Yesterday, I was driving to my hometown, and a flow of marketing ideas popped with excitement and made me feel like I am the guru of marketing when just a day or two before, I was exhausted of ideas. I remembered the saying, "understand your body and mind." Meaning everyone will face something that makes them excited, angry, fearful, or other kinds of feelings. Humans are emotion machines, and I am thankful to be able to recognize these emotions and the state of my mind. Knowing yourself will help you access the desired state of mind by making simple tweaks.

**"Understand your emotions to access the
desired state of mind."**

3/19/2021

Inversing…

I was listening to Charlie Munger explaining the inverse phenomenon, and I was fascinated by how simple and fundamental it is to our decision-making. The concept is taken from mathematical inversion. So basically, instead of asking ourselves, how would we get rich? Or how can we build a successful business? We ask, what can we do to be poor? And how would the business fail? Once we know the inverse to the main question, we know what actions we need to avoid. Simple, but a very effective way to reach the desired destination. When we ask ourselves how we can get rich, for instance, the answers might be complex, but when we ask ourselves how we can be poor, the answer becomes simple and profound. Answer to how to be poor: Spend more than what you gain, and do not invest.

Inversion can also be applied to questions like, how can we be happy? Inverse the question. How can we be miserable? Be around negative people, and develop bad habits.

Humans tend to complicate things as it allows them to escape reality as if an outside high force coming from somewhere is the blame for our situation. However, some mental tools can help us simplify these things.

"Inverse your future life/business to avoid it."

5/28/2021

We officially opened the restaurant!

After more than a year of planning and six months of construction, the restaurant is open. I am proud of what the restaurant turned out to be, considering the poor agency that designed the restaurant, coronavirus, financial constraints, and many other things. Though I thought we would reach our target sales from the day we opened (same expectations from the first day we opened the food truck), sales are moderate but are gradually increasing.

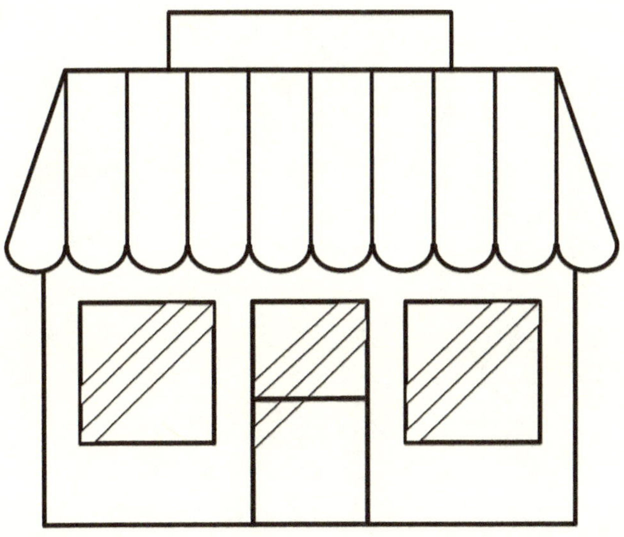

CHAPTER 9

2021 VENTURES, GOALS, AND REFLECTIONS

Opening day & Marketing:

When we opened the restaurant, we sent out invitations to our loyal customers and some bloggers to spread the word, which positively affected the restaurant sales. We wanted to do a special opening, but we did not have enough cash to execute them. And so, we focused on digital advertisements and our loyal customers. I have said that before, but I will say it again, location is the main game, especially for services. Thankfully, when we picked the location, we exerted tremendous effort to search for the right location. And so, the location has and will play a major role in sales.

Operation:

We knew that operating a restaurant was different from a food truck. We had to make adjustments and improvements to fulfill the restaurant requirements, such as cleaning frequency, preparation, working times, and presentation. It introduces more complexity to the business. When we open another food truck, we would be duplicating the systems developed from the previous food trucks. However, in the restaurant case, many things were new to us, and we had to adapt.

Operation Cost:

That is what keeps me awake every night. How much overhead cost can we bare, and will our estimates be accurate? Because things change when you start operating. You might need more labor; electricity is costlier, unsuspected food waste, and the rent is high. I am currently really worried that the cost might slip out of hand. I am trying my best to maintain the cost by optimizing our resources and being more efficient.

5/29/2021

The thought of quitting and moving to Riyadh

I have been away from my family for more than 12 years now, and I have been trying to get closer to my family since I came back from the US after graduating from University. But, I have not found the right opportunity to do so. Time has passed, and since I started working in Saudi Aramco in 2016, I have explored different options that failed to see the light.

I have always put a condition on things that I want to have. So, when trying to move to Riyadh, I told myself that I would move to Riyadh only when I found the right opportunity. And I have not found that opportunity yet. But, after five years since I started working in Saudi Aramco, I am thinking of quitting and moving on with my life while I am not married and do not have many life commitments. The other thing motivating me to move to Riyadh is the flock of people moving to Riyadh in pursuit of better opportunities. Riyadh is becoming the hub for business, from startups to giant companies. Many people from all over Saudi are also moving to Riyadh for better living standards.

Fear of losing versus fear of missing out constrains my moves as if I lose or win without really considering what I want, and that is to get closer to my family, whom I have not been living close by for years because of education and work. I have reached my limits, and I need to make a decision.

I had a meeting once with my manager at work, and he mentioned something that rang a bell in my head. He said, "Abdulrhman, you are so calm, and at your position, you need to know everyone, and everyone needs to know you." He did not say it as a compliment. But I knew that he meant I don't have fire to grap management's attention. He was right; my current job for me was a temporary destination for a future destination. Though I have the fire inside me, it did not find its fuel in my current job. I knew how business has made me feel and how satisfying it is. The business has not left motivation for my stay. And now, with my family being far from where I am, it accelerates my desire to move on.

5/31/2021

Ecosystems…

Ecosystems are the main ingredient of a prosperous life. Some might understand an ecosystem as a culture, but it is much bigger. I came to understand what ecosystems mean after reading "the great mental models volume 2," which delves into life examples that emphasize the importance of ecosystems. One example that I will share here is the elephant example. Elephants are endangered because of habitat destruction, which is combated by artificial insemination. However, artificial insemination reduces the space elephants need to roam and have social ties because they are captives. In turn, this reduced the elephant's mortality and did not help in preserving elephants' lives.

What if, instead of interfering with the natural system, we provided the ecosystem that elephants need to grow in number and prosper. Instead of using artificial insemination, we provide the space, community, and environment that elephants want. Without a doubt, elephants will be saved from the probability of being extinct. Though it is obvious when put that way, it has struck me how important an ecosystem is and how it can be understood incorrectly. An ecosystem is so powerful that it is misperceived.

Take Football, for instance; a good coach is someone who does not focus on the prize but builds an ecosystem that drives the team to win the prize. A successful restaurant will not live long if there is no system that it revolves around, whether for workers, food development, cleanliness, and so on…

I know an ecosystem is not new, but it has a much bigger mindset; it should include continued improvement. No ecosystem is perfect; building or allocating an ecosystem has a much greater cause and objective.

**"Ecosystem is much bigger than a goal.
It is the preservation of life."**

6/1/2021

Pursuing masters…

When I failed multiple ventures, I started looking for jobs in Riyadh that met my goals. I needed to move to Riyadh because it is where my family lives, and I think it is the country's future. I have found different job posts on LinkedIn, which mostly required or favoured an MBA holder. Though I was and still think that universities consume money while providing minimum value, and they are not developing fast enough to meet the market requirements. However, companies want to make sure that the person they are planning to higher understands business, and an MBA can be seen as proof. So after the failures, I decided to ensure that I had the certificates needed to be admitted to the desired job.

When I searched for schools, I wanted to ensure that the school was reputable and had a great online programs. I also found that a master's in business analytics is highly sought after in the job market. So I decided to pursue a Master's in business analytics.

I believe the application journey was a bit tiring. Trying to apply for more than one university by filling out each university application and asking mentors and work colleagues to send a letter of recommendation.

Is the investment in studying at a university worth the money? What is the ROI? If I were to spend it on a stock or a company, wouldn't it be worth more? I honestly do not know. But, I know that investing in yourself is the best investment. Because when you are investing in yourself, you increase your value that nobody can trade but yourself.

**"Invest in yourself, and upskill yourself.
Do not wait for others to do that for you."**

6/13/2021

Venture Capital....

After exploring many opportunities and trying to find the right opportunity, I realized that investing and analyzing opportunities are in my genes. I enjoyed the process, even though I failed at many business opportunities. I wanted to develop something that is part of the future and unique. It was an exercise to look for something better than what I found. Since I had limited money and time to see which one had a higher potential, I had limited chances, meaning I was either all in or out. My blood started rushing with the thought of joining a venture capital and hopefully starting one in the future.

I searched for established firms in Saudi that is active in that field. Then I started approaching the heads of these firms, expressing my desire to join their team. Only one of 4 showed real interest and asked to meet. The meeting went well; he was understanding and excited for me to join. However, he did not know how to set up a proposal because he believed I was overqualified, and requested me to meet another Associate who should see how I could contribute to there VC firm. However, the associate was interviewing me, and I was not prepared mentally. The associate was also a bit intimidating. I felt like I was being challenged and interviewed simultaneously because it is fairly difficult to challenge the interviewer back because you might fall into the mind game trap. Even at the end of the interview, when I asked for the path forward, he replied with a demoralizing tone, "we might get back to you."

At that point, I felt like I had failed. I was answering questions, but my responses did not interest the interviewer. Will I succeed in joining a VC? Who knows.

I think joining a VC is like jumping the ship. It is not an easy decision, but if it comes true, I believe it will be a great opportunity for me to be the investment field.

6/18/2021

The idea of not knowing…

It is frustrating sometimes not to know where we will be tomorrow. Sometimes it feels like you are running toward a wall; other times, it feels like running in the desert, wasting time and energy. That is the life of an entrepreneur. Sometimes I want to sell the business and start over in a new venture and different industry.

My mind is running a lot of different scenarios such as bankruptcy, fear of missing out on available opportunities, exhaustion, etc… I cannot forecast what tomorrow holds for me or the business. My decision-making has become slow because I fear making mistakes that jeopardizes the business.

How do you deal with not knowing? How do you accept that you don't know and that you will figure it out? I remember Ray Dalio talking about it in his Principles book; he stressed making sure we know what we do not know. Take, for example, predicting when will the stock market crash. Nobody knows, and nobody can predict when the stock market will crash. However, we have indicators that can help us to understand where the market is going. So here, we do not know when the stock market will crash, but we can forecast the conditions. Is it going to take a year, two, or a couple? Nobody knows. And I think that is the key to how we see the future; we should have metrics that allow us to see if we are getting closer to our goals.

Mentally it is confusing; the idea of not knowing is overwhelming. It makes one wonder and expects failure, which is hard. I cannot tell you how hard it is, but it feels like a mystery and a puzzle that will either reward you in the end or bite you hard. The idea of not knowing forces you to accept losing. There is no recipe for overcoming the "not knowing" phenomenon. It is the nature of life. We cannot know everything.

> **"Live with what you know, and reconciliate**
> **with what you cannot know."**

6/19/2021

Sharing lessons

Sharing knowledge is difficult. When I find myself in a position to chip in and share an experience, I ask myself if it is worth it? Sometimes it feels like we are just talking as if I am playing a role rather than making an impact. Unfortunately, that feeling has forced me to share less of what I know and think. Sometimes I fear the consequences of sparking a heated discussion because I oppose someone else's opinion, even if I feel that my opinion is supported by knowledge and experience.

In many of my discussions, I feel that we are fighting for who is right rather than what is right. How can you change the atmosphere of a discussion if the other person is not cooperating? We both know that searching for what is right should not be personal; it has to be about us and how we can protect ourselves from being wrong. I believe that I am vulnerable to being wrong, so I tend to share less and express less than I want to. I believe that I also fear feeling embarrassed if the other person does not like what I say. I fear turning a discussion into a toxic argument.

However, our hand fingers point at ourselves before it pointd to others. We must understand that facts are true, but everything else is changing. So, if we do not share what we know now, it might be something we could share tomorrow. When discussing a heated matter, we need to develop a shield for ourselves from the reaction of others. A shield that will allow us to process, understand and share what we think openly and respectfully.

"It does not matter who is right; what matters is what is right."

6/23/2021

Ego State...

I have read "Games People Play" by Eric Brene, a great book on how people communicate with each other from a phycological aspect. Eric describes that people's relationships and communications are games in different forms. Some are commonly more than others, like when someone says "Hi," you respond with "hi," which can be in different languages and forms depending on the culture, religion, region, etc...

In essence, we as people play games with each other, and unless we individually play along, our relationships die. Every person has a game to play, whether a brother who should be there when his other siblings need him, a father who is trying to raise a child, or a professional who plays a role in a team.

Eric explains that people have three ego states, parent ego state, which is a directive state where people tend to be like a parent raising a child. The second state is a mature ego state, where people tend to be moderate and treat others equally. The third state is a child ego state, where people are playful and free of strings.

Eric describes that smart people know how to jump from one ego state to another depending on the situation and games we play. Take a child trying to play with the stove, for example. The best way to ensure the child's safety is to be directive and in the parent's ego state. If you have an employee trying their best to achieve higher goals, being in a parent ego state won't work. However, being in a mature state will be more supportive and allows the person to be motivated.

Another example is when people get burned out from working hard and neglecting their needs, they go out and have fun. In that stage, we try to be in the child's ego state, free of worry and happy.

We cannot always be children, mature, or parents. We have to play the game right to win rather than having a "game over" in our relationships.

**"Mature ego state is hard, but it is the state
where we should be most of the time."**

12/17/2021

Dhando Investor..

"Dhando Investor" is a great book written by Mhonish Pabri. The book explains a simple investing strategy that he describes as "dandho investing." In the early days of Indian migration to the united states, the Patel family was relatively poor with minimum assets to their name and were exploring options to start a new life in America. Patel found a hotel that was sold at a low price since the hospitality market was under market stress and was barely surviving. However, Patel saw the investment in a different angel. He calculated how much it would cost him to buy the hotel (say $1 million), which is at a discount. Then he decided to have his family operate the hotel and dedicate one of the hotel rooms to accommodate his family. In that structure, Patel reduced his investment risks, as he would either generate high returns or lose but not much. The

Patels operated the hotel, which means they will not have the overhead of paying a salary. And, as a bonus, they will have a place to live without paying rent.

The Patels were very successful in their investment and bought many hotels in the subsequent years. The families that followed the Patels copied the Patels' strategy and applied it in hotels, gas stations, and so on, which Mhonish Pabrai describes as the Dhando investing strategy, where your odds of winning are high, and even when losing, you do not lose much. It is the same as the value investing concept, but the Dhando investor differs in minimizing the risk of losing. Warren Buffet also describes a similar concept in his investment style: taking a margin of safety.

While studying in the US, I saw many Indian families operating gas stations and hotels in different cities. And, when I read the book, I understood why that was so. The Dhando investing strategy is an interesting way of looking at investing and business. Our behavior usually forces us to look at the fundamentals of a business, and once we conclude, we either pursue the investment or pass. What if we became like Dhandoo investors and add a margin of safety in our analysis? Our chances of succeeding will be much higher, and losing risks will be minimum.

> **"Dhando investing is, in essence, value investing with the consideration of a margin of safety."**

2/4/2022

Sell…..

I have been thinking of selling the food truck business for awhile now. Though we have built a brand, introduced new products, expanded, and developed a Franchising system. It is disappointing to be giving up after all these years and developments, but it is also non-business like to ignore the signs after taking an outside view of the business. I was looking at the income statement for the past three years, and it shocked me that the net profit three years ago was almost double last year's net income. Expenses for everything have by climbing up and up every year. Fortunately, we are coping with the changes. However, the projections are not optimistic. It is either the franchising model succeeds and we sell many franchises, or we are screwed because expenses will still go up, and we won't be able to keep up with it. Think of it this way, if expenses go up, we can be more efficient (hence expansion) or raise our prices.

I think of where we can go if we continue, and I think of the downside if things do not work out. It is not easy to know when you are biased, how you see your business, and when you can be more rational. It is like your born child; you cannot let it go. However, children grow, and they have to leave the house eventually. So the struggle of being rational on whether to sell a business that you own depends on the profitability of the business, and the present value of the free cash flow generated compared with the payout period. So even if you are making profits, the return on investment can be less valuable than if you cash out.

Did you know that most restaurants fail within three years?! It is brutal. It is estimated that around 33% of startups prosper, which means that 67% of startups fail. Entrepreneurs are optimistic and would not consider the stat when opening a business because we are prone to convince ourselves that it won't happen to us. But statistics are more real than how we feel. So that stat also gives more weight to the selling decision. It has been five years now since we started the business. There are a lot of memories that took a big part of who I am today and how I think. So it is really hard to let go.

"Being rational is not easy, but acknowledging the situation and addressing an outside-inside view can be a process to help you get there."

4/26/2022

Phantom

I have read "Phantom in the Brain," a book written by Ramachandran, who is a neuroscientist. The book revolves around people who lost a body part such as a hand or leg but still believe that the part is still attached to their body and they can use it! You would think that they are crazy. Not the neuroscientist. The brain is fascinating and tricks those people into thinking they still have their body parts. So, Ramachandran accepted to see certain people suffering from the same misconception. In one case, those who lost their hand but still believe the hand is still there came to see the scientist because their relatives brought them. This person sat in front of the scientist, and while in conversation, the scientist drank a hot drink. The scientist then asks the patient to hold the drink with his phantom hand. In his perception, the patient held the cup, though, in reality, the cup was still idle on the table. Ramachandran then holds the cup and pulls it towards his side to see how the patient reacts. Surprisingly, the patient expresses discomfort as if the scientist is pulling his phantom hand away.

How did Ramachandran treat the patients? He knew that neurals were connecting in a way that made the patient believe he still had his hand. So the scientist invented a tool that mirrors the patient using his phantom hands. The patient then realizes that the phantom hand is real and that the patient does not have his hand. The neural connections then redesign themselves due to the new realization.

It is amazing how the brain works. I realized from the book that we can work in our favor or be our enemy. Think about it from an ability perspective. How often have we told ourselves that we cannot do something or cannot achieve our goals? Phantoms can be created by our own doing. But in reality, our brains are so powerful that they can create positive phantoms that work in our favor.

"Phantom is the creation of our brain. By adopting positive behavior and encouraging thoughts, we can create unstoppable phantoms that allow us to be successful."

4/28/2022

Franchising and market stress….

We had two meetings with potential franchisees, and these talks did not advance further. One would wonder if the business is not attractive or the business environment is not compelling because of inflation.

When I look at our business, the story is intriguing for a food truck that started from home and developed and expanded to make a name for itself. However, that wasn't enough for franchisees to take the risk. We depend on the franchising model to lift us to the second level. Competition in the food and beverage industry is like a blood bath; we are seeing new brands emerging with new concepts that make the F&B landscape changes rapidly. The capital investment needed to start an F&B business has also increased drastically, making individual investors not interested in entering the market.

Just in the first quarter of 2022, some suppliers have increased the prices twice! This has never happened to us since we started the business in 2017. The increase is mainly due to inflation that is eating up the world. We did see the increase at the beginning of 2022, so we had to reconstruct the menu prices. It was not easy but necessary.

It is said that food is not affected by economic downturns because "people cannot stop eating." Though this is true to some extent, the food industry itself is not affected, but businesses within it get a hit. So many businesses cannot survive in a downturn because their operation expenses cannot keep up with the market, customer behavioral change due to market challenges, and many other reasons. The sector as a whole will prosper for sure, but it is not true that businesses in the food industry do not close down in stressed markets.

> **"It would be extremely smart to develop a strategy for combating stressed markets, rather than becoming a firefighter during business stresses."**

4/30/2022

I am still trying to reignite my confidence and entrepreneurial spirit. The money and the time spent on failed business ideas have left a scar. I know that a positive person can say that these failures should be viewed as experiences, but in reality, they are failures whether we like it or not. It was not one business but many business ventures; vertical farming, manufacturing, e-commerce, recreation, and health services.

When I look at businesses today, I am more cautious and doubtful. I have changed my analysis strategy more than once. I have developed business plans to construct a foundation for those businesses. This is my greatest asset, the knowledge of business key drivers.

Statistical figures show that 90% of startups fail in the first year, which is a staggering figure. Anyone who wants to be an entrepreneur must stop and think. If a doctor tells a patient that 9 out of 10 die from operation X, the patient will think twice before agreeing to take the risk of doing the operation.

News is very misleading, many would promote the financial freedom that can be gained from having your own business, but the news only prospects the good side of the business and neglects the side that would make entrepreneurs think twice before getting into the business. Do not fall prey to such misleading news. Though it is inspiring, I believe the best source for understanding how businesses succeed is reading biographies of successful entrepreneurs. When you read their biographies, you would know those entrepreneurs went through stressful times that could have killed their businesses. But, luck was on their side, and their business prospered.

Business is brutal, which is why you must always think that you are at the edge of losing your investment, as if your back is put against the wall, and you must take drastic measures to build and develop your business. When you start generating profits, invest those profits in long-term assets such as real estate and stocks of dividend-paying companies. And, to expand your business, fund it through investors. That way, you reduce the chance of losing everything if the market does not favor you.

"Business is brutal, and news is misleading. Think for yourself and do not let others inject an unrealistic view of entrepreneurship."

5/1/2022

Focus is a blessing…

I have learned the importance of focusing the hard way. I have spent a lot of money and time evaluating businesses neglecting the business I built that was generating profits and expandable. I know "neglect" is an exaggeration because we have developed the business from branding and customer reach. However, focus requires more than just expansion. The focus would mean tackling every success factor of the business.

The main issue was my strategy when I started the food truck business. I intended to generate cash from that business and use the cash to build a different business, forgetting that the food industry is big and has a lot of room to build a strong business. Many food brands in the Saudi market exploded to build a strong name for themselves, and some have listed their brand in the stock exchange, such as Burgerizer. If our business strategy was focused on being a leading brand in the Saudi market, and

I mean focus on that aspect, the results would have been much better. Luck is also needed to have better results.

Focus is not something easy to do because the world today has many distractions. If I told you today to pitch me an idea for a business, your mind would be exploding with ideas. Whether these ideas are good ventures or not is another discussion. But, all you need is one idea with a recipe for success, an idea that will always keep you interested in building a conglomerate. If you take the biggest business in the world, they started with one idea. Take Netflix, for example, to disrupt the movie industry. Google, to build the best search engine in the world. Facebook, to build a social platform that everyone in the world uses. These businesses currently have many within sub-businesses, but they would not have reached where they are today if they were not focused on the main business.

"Focus is a blessing. Do not get distracted by thinking of building a conglomerate from day one. Make the current business hard to break first."

CHAPTER 10

RAISING THE WHITE FLAG

7/9/2022

We have sold the restaurant…

After operating the restaurant for more than a year, we had to let go of the restaurant. It was very expensive to operate the restaurant. The main mistake that we learned from the restaurant is operational costs.

Before we decided to build the restaurant, we developed profit estimates to assess the business feasibility. I remember saying, "the restaurant numbers are intriguing, even if expenses increase higher than expected." Unfortunately, our estimates were optimistic. The restaurant's revenue was barely making us break even with our cost. So, six months ago, I had to take the rational decision and offer the restaurant for sale. When we first put the restaurant for sale, we asked for what we believe is a fair price. However, the market is driven by supply and demand, so we had to reduce our price by 70%. Even after we reduced the price, It took us six months to find a serious buyer. I am grateful that we have sold the restaurant. It is a decision that I am proud of. The rent was high, and the restaurant sales were stagnant. The restaurant had to be sold.

The two mistakes that we had made when we opened the restaurant:

1. Our food concept was fast – pick and go. But the restaurant we built was big and had so much unneeded space. We thought our customers would love to stay and eat in the restaurant. But, that contradicted our food concept, which worked, so a bigger space meant a higher rent. We should not have moved away from our food concept, and we should have stuck through and focused on the pick-n-go business model with minimum space.

2. The restaurant rent was very high. It was around 10% of our total revenue when our supply cost increased rapidly. We thought at first that the restaurant's location would generate high revenues. We did not know that sales would be moderate and stay moderate for a long time.

Though it might seem obvious to us by now that we took the wrong decision when we chose a big restaurant, we would not have come to the realization had we not operated the restaurant. Stay with what works, and know your customer's behavior before making any decision. Do not impose on your customers what you want them to do, because they will do what they want at the end of the day. Make sure your strategy when expanding or building a business is to lower costs as much as possible and take a margin of safety (20%) to be ready for challenging realities.

Our overhead cost grew so much that the business could barely generate profits. We had to cut the fat and restructure our business to return to profitability. After we sold the restaurant to cover our losses, we also released five employees from their duties. The food trucks will still operate, and hopefully, after we cut the fat, the business will be financially stable and increase our profits.

When I look back and visualize the business journey, I would say entrepreneurship is lonely and brutal. It is like a battle, and in battles there is a 50-50 chance of winning. And, that is why entrepreneurship is not for everyone.

I have learned in business, what I would have not learned in any day-to-day job. The lessons are unforgettable, from how people behave, to handling crises, to managing employees, to marketing, how to operate a business, and how to achieve sustainability. If time brings me back to the starting point, I would have done it all over again because it cultivated who I am today. If I advised anyone about business today, I would ask them to build something they would enjoy working in: a business to which you would devote your energy and time.

www.ingramcontent.com/pod-product-compliance
Lightning Source LLC
Chambersburg PA
CBHW022140150726
47992CB00002B/682